RESCUING

the

PUBLIC SCHOOLS

*What It Will Take
to Leave No Child Behind*

RESCUING

the

PUBLIC SCHOOLS

*What It Will Take
to Leave No Child Behind*

EVANS CLINCHY

Teachers College, Columbia University
New York and London

Published by Teachers College Press, 1234 Amsterdam Avenue, New York, NY 10027

The opinions expressed in this book are the author's own and do not necessarily reflect the opinions of the Institution for Responsive Education.

Library of Congress Cataloging-in-Publication Data

Clinchy, Evans.
    Rescuing the public schools : what it will take to leave no child behind / Evans Clinchy.
        p. cm.
    Includes bibliographical references and index.
    ISBN-13: 978-0-8077-4764-3 (harcover)
    ISBN-13: 978-0-8077-4763-6 (pbk.)
    ISBN-10: 0-8077-4764-5 (hardcover)
    ISBN-10: 0-8077-4763-7 (pbk.)
    1. Public schools—United States. 2. Educational change—United States. 3. Education—Aims and objectives—United States. I. Title.
    LA217.2.C58   2006
    371.010973—dc22
                                                                2006101057

ISBN13: 978-0-8077-4763-6 (paper)
ISBN 13: 978-0-8077-4764-3 (cloth)

Printed on acid-free paper

Manufactured in the United States of America

14 13 12 11 10 09 08 07   8 7 6 5 4 3 2 1

For Blythe
for all things loved and everything important

Contents

Acknowledgments

The Suggested Readings at the end of this book list a few of the people who have helped make this book possible. Some of them are no longer with us, but many are still operating at full steam. Any complete list would fill up the entire book, so I will only mention the most important ones. Just for starters, in addition to all those specifically mentioned in the text, there are Carl E. Lindstrom, Harold B. Gores, Stephen White, William H. Ohrenberger, David Hawkins, William Hull, Harold Howe II, Glenn Steinberg, Norman Elkin, Elisabeth Allen Cody, Patrick J. Mogan, George Tsapatsaris, Larry Myatt, Linda Nathan, Don Davies, Owen Heleen, Robert J. Fried, Seymour Sarason, Monty Neill, and Brian Ellerbeck, my editor at Teachers College Press.

"The School as a Means of Education"

In 1818 at the age of 9, Charles Darwin, the co-creator of the theory of evolution by natural selection, was sent by his father to Dr. Butler's Grammar School in Shrewsbury, England. Here is his description of that experience:

> Nothing could have been worse for the development of my mind than Dr. Butler's school, as it was strictly classical, nothing else being taught, except a little ancient geography and history. The school as a means of education to me was simply a blank. During my whole life I have been singularly incapable of mastering any language. Especial attention was paid to verse-making, and this I could never do well. I had many friends, and got together a grand collection of old verses, which by patching together sometimes aided by other boys, I could work into any subject.
>
> Much attention was paid to learning by heart the lessons of the previous day; this I could effect with great facility learning forty or fifty lines of Virgil or Homer, whilst I was in morning chapel; but this exercise was utterly useless, for every verse was forgotten within forty eight hours. I was not idle, and with the exception of versification, generally worked conscientiously at my classics, not using cribs. The sole pleasure I ever received from such studies, was from some odes of Horace, which I admired greatly.
>
> When I left school I was for my age neither high nor low on it; and I believe I was considered by all my masters and by my father as a very ordinary boy, rather below the common standard in intellect. To my deep mortification, my father once said to me, "You care for nothing but shooting, dogs, and rat-catching, and you will be a disgrace to yourself and all your family."[1]

I'm afraid that Darwin's statement that "the school as a means of education to me was simply a blank" all too accurately encapsulates my own experience of school and college roughly 120 years later. I consider this fact to be a sad commentary not only on what American education—public and private, elementary, secondary, and collegiate—was like back in my own school days but what it is all too often still like today. I thus offer my experiences in school and college, described in some detail in this book's first chapter, not because they were especially unusual but precisely because they weren't.

I hasten to add here that those experiences were not totally uninspiring. At each level from elementary school through college there were occasional bright spots in which I experienced a taste of what the American system of education could and should be, small signs of hope that always somehow managed to ward off total despair.

I found that I was able to carry those occasional signs of hope into the 40 or so years of a subsequent and rather peculiar professional life spent attempting to improve the educational life of students, and especially poor and minority urban students, in our public schools. Indeed, I not only continued to learn more about what was badly wrong with our system of public education, but I also was able to experience more of those signs of hope and even help to create some myself.

In the course of that professional life, I worked in and with some of this country's largest urban school systems—such as those of Boston, New York, Chicago, Buffalo, and Indianapolis—as well as a host of other smaller urban systems such as Providence, Rhode Island; Rochester, New York; Springfield, Lowell, Fall River, and Worcester, all in Massachusetts; and even Berkeley, California, along with a few suburban systems. In each of these cases my cohorts and I managed to create reforms that were sometimes able to last for a good many years despite the established system's eventual, inexorable, and almost always successful efforts to do them in. It is the story of these professional experiences, including detailed descriptions of those hopeful signs, that form Chapters 2 and 3 of this book.

But all these educational and professional experiences only served to raise in my mind the much larger question of how it came to be that we in this country—and, indeed, educators throughout the Western world—created and now continue to practice a system of educating the young that is not only undemocratic but also intellectually, emotionally, and therefore educationally counterproductive. Chapter 4 is an attempt to describe and perhaps to some extent explain how this happened.

But if we are to reinvent our existing dysfunctional system and replace it with a system that is intellectually, emotionally, and educationally productive, if we are going to make those hopeful signs the educational rule rather than the rare exception, we need to be as sure as we can be about what is actually going on in the heads—and, indeed, the hearts—of the young people we are trying to educate.

Fortunately, according to Alison Gopnik, a cognitive scientist at the University of California at Berkeley:

> In the past 75 or so years—beginning in the 1930's with the work of Jean Piaget and Lev Vygotsky—we have seen the spectacular growth of research on cognitive development. And we have in the last 30 years, begun to develop a sci-

ence of children's minds. This new research might be the equivalent of the scientific physiology that has transformed the practice of medicine over the past 150 years."[2]

In Chapter 5, I attempt to describe what this research is telling us about how we might begin to transform our dysfunctional educational system into that new and more productive one.

If we can combine all the hopeful signs with the new research that supports them, I believe we will have laid the foundations of that new system. In Chapter 6, I attempt to spell out in some detail what that reinvented system of education could and should look like. This new system essentially reverses the distinctly undemocratic structure we now have with one that places the educational decision-making power where it belongs, in the hands of the parents, the professional people, and even the older students the system should be serving.

This last chapter thus spells out what I have come to believe are some of the possible solutions to the long-standing and increasingly desperate and intolerable problems of our present system, in short, that reinvented system of public education I believe all America's children, parents, and professionals need and deserve.

CHAPTER 1

Adventures in the Education Trade

When I say that my schooling was similar to Darwin's, I do not mean, of course, that mine was an exact copy of what Darwin suffered. I was not condemned to study only the Latin classics. Indeed, the teachers at my K–5 school in Washington, DC, and my K–8 school in Hartford, Connecticut, were all good-hearted people who certainly did their best to get us interested in what they were trying to teach us. And somewhere along that line I did learn to read, write, and do basic arithmetic, although I do not remember precisely how or when all that happened.

But my teachers basically saw their job as instilling in us students what the curriculum guides of the day said should be instilled, hoping that it would not all be forgotten within the next 48 hours. Which, as in Darwin's case, most of it was. What I do remember most clearly was that day after day most of my classmates and I sat quietly in our rows of desks, occasionally paying attention to what was being said up front but most of us also twitching and squirming with boredom.

Although this was in the late 1930s and early 1940s and therefore in the middle of what the educational historian Lawrence Cremin has called the "progressive era" in American education from 1917 to 1957,[3] my schools offered no art, no music, no theater, no dance, little science, and contained no animals or plants. Crafts were limited to us boys going down to the basement once a week to make footstools.

I do not remember any of my regular classroom teachers ever asking us what we might be interested in learning or allowing us out of the rows of seats that incarcerated us while they stood in front of the class and talked or wrote on the blackboard. The only entertainment we had was provided by my friend Irving Engleman, who in the eighth-grade classes of Miss Ball and Miss Bean would sit quietly at his desk beguiling us by surreptitiously eating his ruler.[4]

There was, however, one of those "bright spots," one most happy exception to this generally uninspiring record. It occurred when Mr. Black, the principal of that K–8 school, took 18 of us eighth graders out of our regular classes and into the school library twice a week and turned us loose to study, carefully guided by him, a range of things we might genuinely want to learn. I think this must have been Mr. Black's attempt at a "gifted and talented" class or track, since we were selected by means of some kind of test. When the results of that test were posted on the eighth-grade bulletin board I was ranked as 17th out of 18, thus enabling me to be just about equal to Darwin's "a very ordinary boy, rather below the common standard in intellect." Irving Engleman's name did not appear on the list.

But whatever drawbacks that class may have had as an example of undemocratic selectivity, for me that brief experience of genuine progressive schooling was a revelation. Mr. Black would ask us questions to elicit what we were thinking about and then would make individual assignments of things we might be interested in studying and reporting on. We would then have vigorous discussions about what each of us was doing. Mr. Black would then challenge us to keep on learning more and more about what we had become interested in learning. This would also include following up on what we had been learning from listening to one another's reports. At the end of the year we were given another test, and this time I somehow came out ranked as number two.

What I remember most vividly, however, was the enormous relief and pleasure I experienced when I was able to leave those regular classrooms and head for that library. "School," I was discovering, did not have to be dreary, boring, and irrelevant to my life.

But—and perhaps most important—I also remember wondering why we 18 had been selected to be in Mr. Black's class, even though it was clear that the test we had taken had something to do with it. It seemed to me that everything we were doing in that library was something that everyone else in our class, very much including Irving Engleman, could and should have been doing back in the regular classes. This, I discovered myself thinking, was what "school" should be all about.

I do not mean here that our teachers should never have tried to "teach" us some of the things in the curriculum guides—some of the basic historical stories and "facts," for instance—and they certainly should have and did introduce us to the heroes of such literary classics as *Tom Sawyer* and *Huckleberry Finn*. Mark Twain, after all, had lived only a few blocks away from this school, and the local branch of the public library was situated in his old house.

I knew as well, I think, that some of my classmates may have enjoyed and profited from much that went on in those classrooms. But for me, the overarching memory is of Mr. Black's largely successful attempts to make a connection between us as inquiring young minds and all the things out there in the vast world of human knowledge that we might become fascinated by, leading us to fall in love with the act of learning. This was in stark contrast to the tedium of our regular classes where for the most part we meekly tried to learn and remember what our teachers told us we should learn and remember.

Moving On

When the time came for me to graduate from my K–8 school, my parents decided that rather than sending me to the local public high school I should be sent to a nearby all-White, all-male, private day (i.e., nonboarding) prep school that was a somewhat modernized clone of the school attended by Darwin. Indeed, it was a school that had actually been founded by two renegade English "public" (i.e., private) schoolmen who could well have come from Dr. Butler's school. This was a school where the "masters" (all male, of course) wore robes, and we students all wore uniforms of school jackets and ties. We had morning chapel every day, "forms" rather than grade levels, and student prefects to help preserve order. Students in the Lower School (Grades 6 through 8) were assigned to wear either the red rose of Lancaster or the white rose of York and thereby every day refight the English War of the Roses. Again, there was no art, no music, no theater, no dance, little science, no plants or animals, and no crafts of any kind.

It was a school where for me the only respite from the travails of Latin, endless trains of historical dates, French verbs, and the horrors of algebra and trigonometry were the "extracurricular" activities—the editorship of the school literary magazine, occasionally school sports, and rifle practice (this being during World War II, so we were presumably being prepared to join the armed forces. I was very good at rifle, both then and later during basic training in the United States Army).

And again, as with my K–8 school, the masters did their best to make the very traditional subject matter come alive, and for some of my classmates—and even for me—they were sometimes successful. My English masters, for instance, introduced us to Eliot, Joyce, and Yeats, all of whom I found profoundly moving.

But in general my academic performance at that prep school was abysmally mediocre and thus truly Darwinian. I must have taken and passed the SAT and College Board tests, but I have no recollection of taking them or how well I did on them. In any event, I went on (right at the end of the European war) from that school to Harvard College.

After one totally mediocre year there (including flunking a psychology course on the physiology of the eye), I escaped by allowing myself to be drafted. I spent 18 months in the army, where I learned what it is like to live in a totalitarian world that allowed for almost no independent thinking and behaving. Despite the fact that, as far as I could see, I made no contribution to the security of my country, this stint did provide me with 3 years of free collegiate education courtesy of a grateful nation's GI Bill.

I returned to Harvard, where it seemed that any White male from any minimally reputable prep school, as in my case, would be automatically admitted. Indeed, I and a good many of my classmates were clearly there not because we were superb academic material or because we were those members of society who most deserved to go to college; we were there because we were of the proper gender (male), ethnic group (Anglo-Saxon), and social class (middle or upper) and because we were graduates of prep schools acceptable to Harvard.

But this was also the era when World War II veterans were either returning to school (as was my case) or getting into college for the first time as a result of the GI Bill. And many of these veterans were not members of the social classes and ethnic groups of the traditional Harvard student. Indeed, my best friend and roommate was a navy veteran from an impoverished single-parent home in the wilds of upstate New York. There were even women in our classes, since Radcliffe College was being phased out and melded into Harvard itself.

But by and large, my experience at Harvard continued to be proof that Harvard and I were not ideally suited to each other. I was totally unprepared to profit from attending an institution inhabited by some of the best academic minds the country had to offer. Rather, I continued to find academic life for the most part excruciatingly boring and largely irrelevant to my life.

There were, however, two of those educational signs of hope. One was a small—15-member—seminar with the poet John Ciardi, who gently induced us actually to live in a poem, to hear it, to feel its rhythms and melodies, to sense its meaning rather than simply analyze and intellectually understand it. All this leading eventually to a personal belief that Yeats's "The Second Coming" may be the finest poem in the English language.

But most especially important was a repeat of Mr. Black's class with the poet and novelist Theodore Morrison. It was a tiny, selective writing class for aspiring authors that I was able to take for 2 years running. In this class Morrison automatically gave everyone an A and then worked individually with each class member to help us begin to discover and write, either fictionally or nonfictionally, about all the things going on in our heads that were really important to us. Morrison would select one of our products to read in class and then open up the class for praise, criticism, and heated discussion.

It was the kind of experience that, as with Mr. Black's class, could and should have been the way most of Harvard's classes were conducted. This continuing discovery of what had genuine educational meaning for me was greatly enhanced by my constant association out of class with my fellow students who were teaching me how to appreciate all the visual and performing arts that had been systematically ignored in my previous school experiences.

Again, I do not mean that large, impersonal lecture courses that attempt to introduce students to the great minds and intellectual achievements of the human species are necessarily a waste of time. I even remember lecture courses I attended that I found stimulating and rewarding, including a Shakespeare course in which we were required to memorize and recite all the soliloquies in *Hamlet* and the opening speech of the Chorus in *Henry V.*

But my main response to such courses was similar to that of the Nobel Prize–winning physicist Murray Gell-Mann, who has criticized this collegiate system:

> I've always thought that university education, including full-scale lecture courses covering the ground of well-known subjects on which excellent books have been published, are simply an illustration of how the universities have failed to adapt, after 500 years, to the invention of printing.
>
> [In medieval times,] books were published by having a lector read his manuscript to a roomful of scriptores, who wrote it down. Many of the students at the university were too poor to buy books produced by this expensive method, so at the university a theology professor would read his book to the students, who would act as their own scriptores and write down what the teacher said.
>
> With the invention of printing, this system became obsolete, but the universities have still not noticed that, after more than 500 years. Of course, a lecture can serve very important purposes: it can convey brand-new information, along with the exciting character of that information. A dramatic lecture can serve to present the speaker as a role model to the people in the audience.
>
> I have nothing against the occasional lecture. But the idea that at each college and university some professor has to give a series of lectures covering the ground of well-known subjects such as electromagnetic theory on which excellent books have been published, seems totally insane to me. If professors really want to assist learning, they can answer questions when students are stuck, assign challenging problems and fascinating reading, and give occasional exciting talks. . . . *In brief, they can serve as resources for students engaged in the complex, adaptive learning process* [emphasis added].[5]

Which, of course, is precisely what Mr. Black was doing in that library and Ciardi and Morrison were doing in those Harvard classes.

Although it took a special meeting of some mysterious board to decide that my still completely mediocre academic attainments would enable me to graduate from Harvard, I found myself suddenly thrust into a big, buzzing, very "real" world I knew almost nothing about. I had spent 16 years in conventional, middle-class academic schooling and those 18 months in the specialized, authoritarian world of the military, and I possessed only a BA in English. All told, I was clearly unprepared for any useful occupation.

I certainly did not have the slightest desire to continue being academically educated to become a lawyer, doctor, businessman, or professor. And I equally most certainly did not have the skills to get a well-paying job as a plumber, carpenter, electrician, chef, construction worker, or auto mechanic. But I now had actually somehow to earn a living, to get a job and get paid for doing some honest work. The only job I could imagine for which I might be even minimally qualified was a newspaper reporter.

In part through family connections, I lucked into being a cub reporter (at $35 a week) and then eventually a police reporter (during the day) and the music, drama, and dance critic (at night) on a daily newspaper in Hartford. Having grown up leading the sheltered life of a Waspish middle-class prep school/Harvard College lad, I was suddenly tossed during the daylight hours into a world of cops and villains, all of us caught up in a politicized justice system often ruled by comically inept and venal judges and prosecutors and inhabited by sleazy defense lawyers and often unjustly convicted defendants—a daytime world, in short, that I found utterly fascinating. At night, I reveled in the equally rich world of high culture and the performing arts, that world I had learned about from associating with my college friends. All in all, there could hardly have been a better way to be genuinely educated, to begin to learn what life out in that so-called real world was in fact all about.

A year or so into my stint on the newspaper, however, the editors in their wisdom decided that the field of public education warranted the assignment of a full-time (or at least full-day-time) reporter, the first ever in the state of Connecticut. Their eyes lighted upon me, as they thought, quite erroneously, that I was somehow being wasted on my beloved police beat. I wrote a passionate three-page memo explaining why I was the last person on earth who should be assigned to cover "education." The reason being, I wrote, that my own educational experiences from first grade, through elementary school, prep school, and Harvard College had convinced me that "schooling" as practiced by most of the educational institutions in this country could rarely if ever be anything but boring, intellectually stifling, and quite irrelevant to most if not all of any young person's legitimate concerns as a thinking, feeling, developing human being. I knew, of course, that some people did not share my loathing of "school" and had even enjoyed and profited from at least parts of their schooling, as, indeed, I had during those few "bright spots."

Aha, said the editors, just the person we are looking for, someone who is intensely skeptical of formal schooling. My heartrending cries thus fell upon deaf editorial ears, and I became most unwillingly and against my better judgment professionally involved in the world of American public education. I spent the following 6 years covering local school board meetings and state board of education meetings and sitting in and reporting on what was going on in classrooms all around the state (including back at my old K–8 school, where there was now no class similar to Mr. Black's).

While I had been a total mediocrity as an academic, I was more successful as a newspaperman. As it happened, my old alma mater, Harvard, instead of having a journalism school, had established something called a Nieman Fellowship program that enabled practicing newspaper people to apply and be selected to spend a year there being very minimally paid to study whatever they wanted to study. So, after 8 years on my newspaper, I did apply and was accepted.

Instead of being subjected as I had been during my 4 college years there to a raft of courses dictated by the scholars who established the academic curriculum, this time I was allowed to spend an entire academic year exploring any course I was interested in and conferring privately with any faculty member I thought might satisfy my burgeoning curiosity. We Niemans did not have to take any tests or write any papers or go through the hoops of getting any advanced degrees. I was once again back in Mr. Black's and Mr. Morrison's classes. And one of the courses I avidly took was in physical and cultural anthropology, thus encouraging what has become a lifelong fascination with the dramatic story of human evolution.

I then moved on to being a writer and program officer at an educational subfoundation of the Ford Foundation, now spending time in schools and classrooms all over the country. This was a time when the foundation was encouraging what it hoped might be a revolution in the public schools through such reforms as team teaching and a new kind of school organization that called for the differentiated grouping of students into large classes for lectures, middle-sized groups for conventional teaching, and smaller classes for more individual work. These reforms required the redesign of existing school buildings or the design of brand-new schools and led to the idea of "open space" schools in which the walls between classrooms were removed to provide instructional flexibility. Unfortunately, this idea became confused with "open" or informal, developmental schooling, with which, as we shall see, it had absolutely nothing in common.

Although my job at the foundation was to seek out and assist creative educational efforts wherever I could find them, the vast bulk of those schools and classrooms turned out to be simply clones of the ones I had endured in Mr. Black's school, at my prep school, and as an undergraduate at Harvard. My experience matched that of Sophie Haroutanian-Gordon, an education professor at Northwestern University, who has said:

> Pick a classroom in this country or most any other—elementary, secondary or collegiate—and stop for a few minutes. Chances are you will see the teacher lecturing or demonstrating to the students rather than probing their ideas through

questions. Even if you do observe the teacher questioning, chances are the aim is to determine whether the students have acquired some predefined competence or understanding rather than to conduct an open-ended exploration of their thoughts.[6]

It did not take very long for my old educational questions to resurface, but I now came to ask them in even broader form: If the schooling offered in the classes of Black, Ciardi, and Morrison had been so rewarding, why isn't it the way all America's public school classes are conducted? And the inevitable question followed: How and why did we create the counterproductive educational system that I not only experienced myself but also saw all around me as I traveled across this country?

Two Additional Great Educational Experiences

As those Ford Foundation years continued, I began to grow weary of continually observing how the schools I was visiting and reporting on seemed so resolutely dedicated, as mine had been, to making sure that their students rarely had a chance to use their minds well and become enthralled by such use. Perhaps it was time, I thought, to try to do something about it. But what was I equipped to do? Not much, it seemed to me.

But once again fate or something like it came to my rescue. Mainly as a result of my Ford Foundation work and my passion for the human evolutionary story, in the early 1960s I was invited to become part of what was called the "curriculum reform" movement. This movement went into high gear in 1957 when the Russians launched their Sputnik satellite and, as Cremin puts it, "a shocked and humbled nation embarked on a bitter orgy of pedagogical soul-searching."[7]

One result of this orgy—and its accompanying charges of educational failure on the part of the public schools—was the launching of large-scale curriculum reform efforts in all the major academic disciplines. This movement, led by a coalition of concerned university scholars and school people, had actually begun in 1951 in the field of mathematics, but it quickly spread into physics, biology, and chemistry and then into the field of social studies, combining history, anthropology, and the social sciences.

The aim of this movement was to redress the perceived failure of the public schools to produce highly qualified, well-educated people, especially in the fields of science and engineering; people able to meet the national challenge posed by the Soviet Union being "ahead" of us in both the space and educational races. The way to do this was to marshal the best academic scholars from the colleges and universities to decide what students should learn in each of the traditional subject matter disciplines. The scholars would then team up with forward-looking people in the schools to revitalize the entire instructional program of an American public educational system that was responsible, as one critic put it, for "the unsatisfactory state of our life and culture."[8]

One of the leading curriculum development entities was called Educational Services Incorporated (ESI), now called Education Development Center (EDC) which had been created by two Massachusetts Institute of Technology physics professors, Jerrold Zacharias and Francis Friedman, to build a new high school physics course (the Physical Science Study Committee, or PSSC, course). ESI, however, went on to promote other curriculum development efforts in mathematics, biology and chemistry, including three that it actually ran itself— a junior high science program, an elementary school science program, and a K–12 program in social studies.

It was ESI that offered me the opportunity to join this movement. So, in part as a result of my anthropological/evolutionary passion, I found myself being the administrative and educational director of the ESI elementary school social studies program that was eventually produced as a curriculum package as Man, a Course of Study (or MACOS) under the overall direction of the distinguished cognitive psychologist Jerome Bruner.

Although this program was a typical academically oriented reform effort, it would not be accurate to say that it was completely antiprogressive. While it did give paramount importance and control to the university scholars and their ideas about what should be studied, there was considerable pedagogical attention paid to how such ideas might be conveyed to students. Indeed, Bruner himself and other developmental psychologists were involved in this process. And those of us responsible for the actual preparation of "instructional units" were very much concerned with how best to go about this task.

This social studies program, however, did follow the basic curriculum reform model and was thus run by two groups of people. There were, first, the university scholars, including Bruner, who made the fundamental decisions about what students were supposed to learn and at what level—elementary or secondary—they were supposed to learn it. The second group was us nonscholar staff members whose job was to turn that scholarly vision of the world into educational materials that elementary school children and teachers could use in their classrooms.

For instance, we created films of Inuit (Netsilik Eskimo) life, of African primates in their natural habitats, and of the archaeological research that established the origins of domesticated corn agriculture in the highlands of Mexico. We invented hunting-and-gathering games and units on human evolution and the origins of agriculture, settled life, and eventually urban life in Middle America and Mesopotamia and so on.

We ended up during the 5 years I was there spending a great deal of federal and foundation money and accomplishing precious little, if anything, for the elementary school children of this country. Although our educational materials certainly did reflect the latest achievements of the scholarly world, the "instructional units" we were preparing were still essentially based on the traditional information-transmission model of education. That is, we took what the scholars thought were the basic ideas—the so-called structure—of the academic disciplines we were dealing with and tried to develop ingenious and irresistible educational materials that would entice elementary school children to learn what the scholars believed they should learn.

Most of these materials did attempt to be "hands on" in that they were designed so that students had original data and objects to work with. The Netsilik films, for instance, were simply careful ethnographic depictions, without any accompanying narration, of people going about their daily lives—fishing at a stone weir, seal hunting, building an igloo or a sealskin boat, making clothes, preparing and eating meals. Students, then, were asked to be their own anthropologists, trying to understand, to make sense of, a way of life quite different from their own but conducted by people who were also in every fundamental human way just like the students themselves. Or, in studying the origins of settled life in Mesopotamia, students were asked to see if they could make a model of a Marsh Arab reed hut or make a truly workable mud brick and thus begin to understand the challenges the Sumerians faced in building their magnificent temples and ziggurats (or as one student said after repeatedly failing to make a brick that actually held together, "Hey, you know it isn't all that easy to make a good mud brick!").

But in the end, I came to see that what we were doing in essence was shoring up the existing organizational structure and instructional approach by which most Western schools, colleges, and universities have always operated. We were attempting to do to elementary school children exactly what the scholars were themselves doing to students in their own classes at their own institutions, that is, imposing on students precisely the autocratic, top-down, instructional educational system that I and so many others had suffered through for so many years.

I came to believe that this venerable process not only hadn't worked for me in Mr. Black's school (except for that one class) and in most of my subsequent educational experiences (except for the Ciardi and Morrison classes and that Nieman year) but it also was not working for the children we were testing our materials on. While those children in some cases did become intrigued by our materials (such as the Netsilik films), my observational conclusion was that by and large they saw our materials as rather ordinary, not very interesting schoolwork. Only occasionally did I see their eyes light up, as in the cases of the Netsilik films and the mud brick, with a sudden, delighted insight into a way of life different from their own or something that had happened long, long ago.

What I began to understand was that we had things exactly backward. Instead of starting where the children were and carefully and respectfully guiding them to more complicated and demanding intellectual models, we started where the scholars were and hoped that somehow we could succeed in the hopeless task of persuading the children that what they were supposed to learn might actually have some meaning for them.

We also, I later realized, almost completely ignored the profoundly useful contextual school experience of the superb public school teachers who had volunteered to help us test our materials. I can all too well remember instances when a teacher would suggest that we give the students more time to play with the materials or suggested that the materials were simply well beyond the cognitive capacities of most of the students we were trying them on. But we were far too busy satisfying the disciplinary requirements laid down by the scholars to pay proper attention to the teachers' experience and educational wisdom.

We did, however, strenuously resist one idea that was rampant in the minds of many of the scholars involved in the national curriculum reform program. This was the idea of attempting to produce "teacher proof" materials that therefore could not be ruined by what the many of the scholars contemptuously saw as all those ignorant, ill-trained teachers out in the public schools.

Although we ended up spending a great deal of federal and foundation money while accomplishing little, if anything, for this country's elementary school children, for me it was another of the great educational experiences of my life. Indeed, what I was experiencing was simply a more complex, more sophisticated version of what had gone on in Mr. Black's eighth-grade class, Mr. Morrison's class, and during my Nieman year. This time, during the years I worked at ESI, I was receiving an incomparable, mind-blowing education, conducted entirely by being allowed to explore, essentially on my own, but now in concert with the most knowledgeable minds the country had to offer, the entire course of human existence on this planet from the dim prehuman world of our primate ancestors to the busy, buzzing confusion and richness of the world's contemporary cultures.

As with the Nieman experience, I took no courses, sat for no exams, wrote no academic papers in the ordinary sense, and received no advanced degrees, nor was I subjected to instructional units such as the ones we were building for elementary school children. In short, no one "instructed" me. Instead, the scholars I was working with guided my reading, helped me to find answers to my questions, and directed my learning without even realizing they were educating me. And, although I did not really see it at the time, I was always in process, as the contemporary jargon of assessment would have it, of "demonstrating" my level of "achievement", my "authentic understanding of the material," and developing a "portfolio" of my academic accomplishments. These clear manifestations of my supposed level of intellectual/academic achievement were the curricular materials I was in charge of producing.

Indeed, if those materials were not judged to be accurate representations of what the scholars believed to be "true," if what I and my cohorts were producing did not meet the largely unspoken "standards" of the scholars, I was told so in no uncertain terms and, suitably chastened, my colleagues and I had to trundle back to our drawing boards to, as Zacharias was often moved to say, "get it right."

And of course I was being paid to be so educated. If students of any age must be forced to submit to the study of the scholarly disciplines conducted within the four walls of our detached school and university classrooms (which was what we were still essentially expecting our social studies students to be doing), then this was the absolutely perfect, utterly delightful way to go about it. It was the ideal antithesis to all of the educational misery I had endured throughout 16 years of conventional schooling in elementary school, high school, and Harvard College. It is a form of education I can heartily recommend to anyone with several million dollars of federal and foundation money to spend.

A Second Great Experience

But this social studies experience was only the first of my two great educational experiences at ESI. The second came toward the end of those 5 years when I had been imposing scholarly ideas on innocent children and defending what we were doing in the social studies program. It was then that I gradually began to realize that the kind of educational process I was coming to believe in was happening right next door, in one of the other ESI curriculum development programs, called the Elementary Science Study (ESS).

This project had been created in the early 1960s by the aforementioned Francis Friedman and was later led by David Hawkins, a brilliant philosopher of science at the University of Colorado, and William Hull, a supremely gifted teacher and materials designer. Its staffing included such distinguished scholars and educators as the future renowned biologist Lynn Margulis, the psychologist/educator Eleanor Duckworth, and, at times, such educational innovators as the teacher and author John Holt.

ESS was a genuinely progressive group of scholars and teachers who were working with elementary school children in precisely the way I had not been doing in the social studies program. They started where the children themselves were and with what they were interested in learning. This meant developing classrooms that were filled with "things"—concrete objects that the naturally curious children could, in the Hawkins/Hull idiom, "mess about with," a phrase and an idea borrowed from Kenneth Grahame's *Wind in the Willows*.[9] These things might be batteries and bulbs that the children, if they wanted the bulb to light up, had to piece together into a working electrical circuit or balance beams that they had to get to balance and thus begin to understand how the two sides of a mathematical equation, the sides separated by the equals sign, had to balance by being equivalent. Or they might be Cuisenaire rods or attribute blocks that could be fitted together to make intricate patterns that involved not merely counting but figuring out mathematical and logical relationships.

Or they could be gerbils living in a cage who had to be cared for and their biological functions understood if they were to be kept alive, thereby introducing the children to the elementary laws of biology. Or things that the children themselves brought to school—broken clocks and radios and other homely devices that the children could fiddle with and even fix—but only if they figured out how they actually worked. And lots of books connected to the things the children where working on.

"Messing about" in this fashion is also, interestingly, the creative method that Thomas Edison and his collaborative team of inventors practiced at the Edison laboratory in Menlo Park, New Jersey, in the process of producing their more than 1,000 patentable inventions. They called it "mucking in" and called one another "muckers."[10]

In essence, all these activities were laying the intellectual groundwork for the study of the laws of the sciences and logical thinking the children would encounter later and better understand from having messed about with these concrete objects. One of the underlying purposes of this approach was to encourage children, as Eleanor Duckworth puts it, to have "wonderful ideas" about how the universe works.[11] As Duckworth has said,

> In my entire life as a student, I remember only twice being given the opportunity to come up with my own ideas, a fact I consider typical and terrible. . . . I had been excited about ideas before, but they had always been someone else's ideas. My struggle had always been to get in on what I thought somebody else knew and knew to be important.

It was only much later that, for the first time, she had "a sense of what it was like to pay attention to my own ideas."[12]

The teachers in these ESS classrooms were rarely involved in direct instruction, but rather acted as guides and mentors and especially as askers of questions, such as "Why do you think that bulb actually lit up?" and "How would you go about finding that out?" or "What would happen if you forgot to feed the gerbils for a whole week?" These classrooms often appeared to casual visitors as disorganized and as "kids just having fun." But they were in fact carefully structured, with the teachers and children together exploring how a rich collection of concrete materials could help the children not simply to learn but to be captivated by learning.

What the ESS people were doing, I finally began to see, was reviving ideas pioneered in the 1700s and 1800s in Europe by the likes of Robert Owen, Johann Pestalozzi, Johann Hebart, Fredrich Froebel, Alfred Russel Wallace, and Maria Montessori and then in this country in the late 1880s and early 1900s by Francis Parker, Jane Addams, John Dewey, and all the other great progressive educators.

And the ESS people were particularly influenced by what had been happening since the early 1940s in the infant and primary schools of Britain, most especially what had been happening after World War II in the schools of the county of Leicestershire in England, where this kind of schooling was called "open" or "informal" education and the "integrated day" (more on all these progressive explorations in Chapter 4).

The ESS people were also aware of the explosive growth of cognitive and developmental psychology, especially the pioneering work of such psychological giants as Jean Piaget, Lev Vygotsky, Susan and Nathan Isaacs in Britain, and Bruner himself in this country, work that has been followed and expanded upon by a host of current thinkers such as Howard Gardner, Alison Gopnik, and Eleanor Duckworth herself (more on this in Chapter 5).

Eventually, this ESS approach (as well as a visit to the British infant and primary schools) and my own educational experiences at the social studies program convinced me that we had been quite wrong in the scholar-dominated and still largely information transmission approach we had adopted in that program. I suddenly—if belatedly—made the connection between what we were then beginning to call "developmental" schooling and what Mr. Black had been doing in that "progressive" eighth-grade library class in Hartford, what I had experienced at Harvard with Ciardi and Morrison, and also during my Nieman year. And it clearly was the way, I was becoming convinced, that all education in all schools, colleges, and universities—public and private—should be conducted.

CHAPTER 3

An All-Too-Brief Creative Advance into Novelty

Those Leicestershire-inspired ESS classes were part of a brief progressive renaissance of the 1960s and early 1970s, a period when such progressive "open education" schools and classrooms were being created here and there around the country, not only in the private schools but in public schools as well. This rebirth was part of that brief era in American history that saw the great civil rights movements, the desegregation not only of schools but of all public accommodations, the Voting Rights Act, Lyndon Johnson's War on Poverty, and the massive resistance to the Vietnam War—in short, a historical period in which it seemed possible that American society might be entering another truly progressive era comparable to the 1930s, which saw the advent of Franklin Roosevelt's New Deal, Social Security, the Works Progress Administration, and other salutary, welfare state/safety net programs.

It even seemed that we might finally be developing an American political system that was truly democratic, a system that genuinely believed that all its citizens of whatever color or income level deserved fair and equal treatment. There was even the possibility that we might at last be realizing Roosevelt's vision of a nation in which "the test of our progress is not whether we add more to the abundance of those who have much; it is whether we provide enough for those who have too little."[13]

This was also the period when a number of books began appearing that enthusiastically advocated the new progressive educational revolution, including the seminal book on the Leicestershire schools, Joseph Featherstone's *Schools Where Children Learn*, along with Jonathan Kozol's *Death at an Early Age*, Herbert Kohl's *36 Children*, James Herndon's *How to Survive in Your Native Land*, John Holt's *How Children Fail*, Lillian Weber's *The English Infant School and Informal Education*, and Charles Silberman's *Crisis in the Classroom* and his *Open Classroom Reader*.

My opportunity to participate in this rebirth came when in 1964 I was able to propose to William Ohrenberger, then superintendent of schools in Boston, that the Boston system should create within itself a new organizational animal, a special piece of the system to be called the Office of Program Development (OPD), that would serve two purposes.

One purpose would be to act as the research and development arm of the system. This would be accomplished through the creation of what we called an early-childhood-through-grade-12 "model demonstration subsystem" made up of three brand-new, closely linked "experimental" schools—an early childhood/elementary school, a junior high, and a high school. Each of these schools would put into practice the form of developmental schooling appropriate to its level. This meant that the early childhood program and the three higher schools essentially became a single school, with all four units planning and conducting their educational programs together as a single, coordinated, seamless developmental educational experience.

It also meant that all parents voluntarily enrolling a child in the early childhood, kindergarten, or elementary school subsystem programs were guaranteed to have that coordinated, seamless developmental educational experience for their child or children all the way through high school. There would be no educational disruptions or dislocations as students moved from elementary to junior high to high school.

The second connected and concurrent purpose of OPD was to create an Educational Planning Center, which would be responsible for the planning of the raft of new schools that the city was already committed to building. The aim here was to funnel any and all successful developmental "experiments" emerging from the subsystem into the planning of those new schools and thus, as the new schools were put into operation, gradually to transform the entire Boston system.

In this very real sense, then, the combined purpose of the OPD operation was not just to introduce progressive classroom practices in a few specialized schools but to see if it might be possible to revitalize an entire urban school system along progressive lines. This would require not just introducing developmental pedagogical practices in a few specialized schools, but also "progressively" altering the relationship between an urban school system; its teaching and administrative staffs; and most important, its parent constituency, the clients of the system who had been systematically excluded from any real participation in the decision making about the education of their children.

Ohrenberger enthusiastically agreed to this plan and invited me to come into the system to create and direct this new entity, which I did after a visit to the Leicestershire schools to be sure I had a clearer idea of what we should be doing in Boston. So we at OPD in the spring of 1965 began the task of creating the Educational Planning Center and those three new schools in the predominantly African American, low-income community of Roxbury. Since at that time Boston had not yet been ordered to desegregate its schools, these would have to be "de facto" segregated schools with all–African American student and parent bodies—or what in those days were called "disadvantaged minority" students and parents.

In line with the job of the subsystem part of OPD being to conduct educational research and development, we insisted upon and were granted an operating situation that any practicing public school person would see as being the closest thing on this earth to having died and gone to heaven. We had complete administrative and curricular autonomy and thus were able to conduct our selected "experiment" of the Deweyesque, progressive, developmental, integrated-day mode of schooling in all three schools.

I had the power to recruit and select our entire teaching and administrative staffs from anywhere within the Boston system. Although we could have recruited teachers from outside the system, we made a deliberate decision to use only volunteers from within the system to show that the necessary talent and expertise for radical change existed within people inhabiting a perfectly ordinary urban public school system, but that those people had simply never had the chance to practice what they believed in.

I was given the unheard-of power (agreed to by a very cooperative Boston Teachers Union) to visit any classroom in the city to find and pick the people I wanted to staff all three schools—but only if they themselves wished to volunteer to become a part of the subsystem experiment. Or those people interested in becoming a part of the great "experiment" could volunteer on their own (which many of them did), be interviewed by me, and selected or rejected. I would say that my score on the selection of people on the basis of those visits and interviews was at best 50–50—no better than purest chance. That is, some of the people I thought most highly of in the interviews turned out to be mediocre at best, while people about whom I was dubious turned out to be real stars. So much for hierarchical administrative wisdom.

Those people selected or self-selected then had to volunteer for at least 1 year to come and find out if they could work successfully in the new system, during which time their old jobs were held open for them. If either we or they thought they did not work out, they could ask or we could ask them to return to those jobs.

We also had complete fiscal autonomy in the sense that the Boston system provided us our school facilities, paid our teachers their normal salaries, and provided us with all the money for materials and supplies that every other public school got, but we could spend that money in whatever way we decided.

That "normal" school department budget, however, was richly augmented by a large quantity of additional funding from the brand new federal Elementary and Secondary Education Act. This came from using a small part of Boston's allocation under what was then called Title I—now called Chapter I—funding for "compensatory education" for "disadvantaged" poor and minority children. According to the federal Title I guidelines, this money was only supposed to be used to supplement the existing educational programs of the schools attended by disadvantaged children, not to set up and run brand new, wildly experimental schools. That task of "innovation" was supposed to be carried out with funds provided under what was then called Title III. But we in Boston used this Title III money to set up the Educational Planning Center part of OPD.

So far as the Title I funds were concerned, the federal authorities administering the program knew perfectly well that what we were doing with the money did not fit the legislation's guidelines, but they conveniently looked the other way, since they heartily approved of how we were using the money. We used that federal money for several purposes: to add staff to our three schools, primarily in the form of adding such people as curriculum specialists and consultants familiar with or interested in the Deweyesque, progressive, integrated-day approach (including bringing an integrated-day expert over from Leicestershire); to hire a full-time parent activity coordinator for the elementary school and a full-time teacher aide for each classroom, all of them drawn from the school's parent body; to hire a full-time arts-and-crafts teacher and part-time music and dance consultants; to institute our early childhood unit for 3- to 5-year-olds (an educational program the system itself did not offer and therefore could not fund); and to set up our own research unit within OPD to track and "assess" both student and subsystem progress.

But perhaps most important, we used the federal funding radically to alter the life of the subsystem's teachers and administrators. To begin with, class size was limited to 20 students in elementary classes, and at the secondary level we tried to keep it to 15.

Although teacher and administrator base pay was supplied by the school system at whatever step on the salary scale they happened to be, we also used the federal money to do two things: We added money to their pay to fund an additional hour every day for after-school planning and self-directed staff and curriculum development workshops, and for an additional month in the summer, again for continued planning and replanning and for joint and quite mutual exploration and learning sessions with people from local colleges and universities (most notably the Harvard Graduate School of Education). We compassionately did give ourselves the month of August off.

So every subsystem teacher and administrator was paid roughly 20% more than regular teachers in the system, but they had to work longer and harder to get that extra money. In actual fact, since our teachers had always been "dedicated" teachers when in the regular system, we were only really paying them for the extra unpaid time they had always put in anyway. So our subsystem teachers thus were actually paid for and worked what amounted to a regular 8-hour day and an 11-month year, just like normal people.

We also quite deliberately made the decision to locate all three subsystem schools in Roxbury, a section of the city that contained a large percentage of the city's African American population. And the children of many of these families fit the official federal definition of "poor" and "disadvantaged" minority children. Indeed, one thing we wanted to demonstrate was that, given decent, caring, adequately funded schools, African American children who had been labeled "poor" and "disadvantaged" were equally as educable as middle-class White children, a belief that was not widely shared in the Boston system— or in American education in general—at that time.

When I say "we" here I mean the all-White administrative structure of OPD and the subsystem, not the all-White structure of the rest of Boston school system itself and certainly not the all-White Boston School Committee. In 1965 there were no African American or any other minority members of the Boston School Committee or among the upper-level administrators in the system or serving as principals of schools—and, indeed, very few African American teachers anywhere in the system. We recruited every African American teacher we could persuade to join us, and some of these turned out to be our real stars, including several who went on to become among the first African American administrators in the system. But our initial staffs at the three schools were, like the rest of the system, heavily White.

So with all-too-typical White liberal (and racist?) Lords and Ladies Bountiful mindsets, we at OPD descended upon the African American community in 1965 and announced that we were going to create three wonderful schools for the African American parents and children of Roxbury. For our elementary school, we took over a dilapidated school, built in 1873, called the W. L. P. Boardman School, named after a former Boston mayor. Our junior and senior high divisions moved into and took over the nearby Lewis Junior High School building.

The Boardman was not a school high on the African American community's list of favorite schools. Indeed, in 1964, the parents of the African American children attending the Boardman had sued the city to have the school closed down because they considered it dangerously antiquated and uninhabitable. When their suit was turned down, the angry parents and leaders in the African American community organized a protest called Operation Exodus and withdrew many of their children not only from the Boardman but from other schools as well, taking upon themselves the job of transporting their children to predominantly White schools in the city. This left the Boardman with a full staff of teachers (most of whom eventually and voluntarily decided to move to other schools) but with a skeleton crew of only 60 students for a school built to house 200.

And early in pre-OPD 1965, Martin Luther King Jr. had come to Boston and been taken to the Boardman to be shown an example of the terrible educational conditions imposed on African American children in the Boston schools. He was refused admission by the school's custodian, whereupon he commandeered a bullhorn and on the spot organized the greatest civil rights march in Boston history, a march that started in Roxbury and ended with a massive protest meeting on Boston Common.

Learning on the Job

When we at OPD deliberately chose the Boardman for our elementary experiment, we simply and stupidly did not realize what we were doing. We did not ask the African American community and especially the parents of the 60 children in the school whether they wished to have their school taken over by the subsystem or whether they wished their children to have an "open" or "developmental" type of schooling.

This tyrannical, peremptory action on the part of the school system and us OPD types only served to fan the already flaming anger of Roxbury's African American community. Almost immediately after the takeover, the parents of the Boardman children and African American community leaders gathered in the school's basement meeting room to assail OPD and the subsystem's staff for this outrageous behavior.

So the first great learning experience of the Boardman experiment, at least for us OPD "experts," came at the very beginning of that memorable 1965 evening. What business, we were bluntly asked, did we have barging into the African American community and arbitrarily and arrogantly taking over not only one of the community's school buildings but an already existing population of African American children? And without in any way consulting with, asking the permission of, or respecting the wishes and rights of the parents of those children or of the African American community as a whole? Who did we think we were, anyway?

It was a good question. And we had no good answer for it. Who were we and why did we do it? We fairly quickly realized why we had done it—because that was the way we Whites and the Boston school system had always operated. Decisions such as these were always made "downtown" at school headquarters, not out in the neighborhoods and especially not out in African American neighborhoods. It was downtown, after all, where all educational wisdom resided. It was therefore perfectly normal and natural for the wise White people downtown (including us OPD types) to decide that this derelict school out in the wilderness of the African American community would make an ideal location for our experiment.

After all, it was known to be one of the worst schools in the city, having been certified as such by no less than Martin Luther King, Jr. himself. And, since it housed only 60 students, it was obviously a failure. Thus by taking over one of the worst schools in the city and turning it into one of the best schools in the city, we would be proving that it was not the all–African American school population that made a school bad (which was what many of the Whites in the Boston system believed) but rather the kind and quality of the schooling that was offered there. Therefore the community leaders and parents would obviously be delighted to have all these wonderful things happen to their children at the Boardman, wouldn't they?

Well, as it turned out, they damn well wouldn't. The only feeble response we OPD people could come up with was a deeply embarrassed apology, a promise that if any parents wished to withdraw their children we would find them a place at the school of their choice, and the suggestion that, if the community leaders and the parents so desired, we would withdraw from the Boardman and the African American community entirely and put the experimental program at some other school—perhaps an all-White, low-income school in predominantly Irish South Boston, the section of the city that would become infamous as a stronghold of antidesegregation passions?

It was this last suggestion—a not-so-subtle form of educational extortion—that finally turned the tide in our favor. Although the community leaders still grumbled, the Boardman parents decided that if good things were going to happen to anyone's children in the Boston public schools, they might as well happen to their children. We helped those parents who did not wish themselves or their children to be a part of the Boardman experiment to find another nearby school where they would feel more educationally satisfied. The almost 150 empty seats in the school were rapidly filled by neighborhood students whose parents eagerly applied for their admission.

In this very real sense, then, all the parents and students in the subsystem became, like the teachers, volunteers. The children were now attending the Boardman or the Lewis only because their parents wanted them to be there, because the parents had freely chosen to put them there.

So we began. We did several things right off. We abolished corporal punishment, which was still officially practiced in all Boston schools. A second thing we did was to ask the parents at each school to form a parent organization made up solely of parents. No teacher, no director of the school, no member of OPD, no employee of the Boston school system was allowed to attend a meeting of any parent group unless specifically invited by the parents.

The job of the parent group was to act as a watchdog and parent/child advocate group, to protest, to ask any and all embarrassing questions, to put pressure on us school people and fight us, if necessary, for what they wanted. We school system types, if summoned by the parents, would appear at any meeting to answer questions and to explain what we were doing and why, and if the parents still objected, we would stop doing whatever it was they didn't like.

We also made it clear that parents were not only welcome in their schools at any and all times but that we believed that they had to be there. Indeed, we came rapidly to realize that if a subsystem school (or any school, for that matter) was going to succeed it would have to be a joint enterprise between the parents and the professional staff, a truly collaborative partnership seen and understood as such by the parents, the staff and especially by the children in the school. All members of the school community had to feel themselves to be an important, working part of the school, sharing the vision of what the school might become.

We and the Boardman parents created a special parents center in the school, with eternal coffee and doughnuts and staffed by a full-time parent activity coordinator, who had her own children in the school. Each of the eight classrooms in the school also had a full-time parent aide, who also had to have a child in the school, with all these parents thus naturally serving as the daily eyes and ears of the parent group itself. All other parents were urged to come in at any time to visit and to help out with all the educational activities going on in the classrooms, which they most certainly did. Parents were also urged to attend all staff meetings and workshops. Indeed, an official representative of the parents group, in addition to the parent coordinator, was expected to attend all such staff meetings, to play an active role in all the discussions, and to report back to the other parents what went on.

In these ways, then, we tried to make parents full partners in the operation of the school and in the education of their children. Yet even so, we at OPD stopped short of the next step of setting up a system of genuine shared governance, of creating a school governing board made up of elected representatives of the school's parent body, its teachers, and the school's director (the OPD equivalent of principal). We were still too conscious of our charge to forge ahead with our developmental schooling experiment to risk the chance that such a fully empowered governing board might decide that this purpose of the subsystem should be abandoned.

But the parents eagerly took over their new role as equal partners in the subsystem experiment. From what had been that early hostility, both the feeling and the fact of two separate and quite unequal warring camps, there began to grow what certainly looked and felt like not only a genuine partnership but even a warm camaraderie between the parents and the teachers.

Each side slowly began to learn from the other. The key here, I am sure, was the growth of simple and mutual respect. The parents, convinced at the outset that the Boston school system could never be anything but their and their children's enemy, discovered that this did not have to be the case. It was possible, they realized, for Boston school people (both White and African American) to respond to them as just plain human beings, endowed with the same dignity and pride, the same overriding concern for the welfare of their children as everyone else in the world.

We OPD types thus made another great discovery. We learned that these African American parents in the heart of what was then always referred to as the "Black Ghetto," many of them single parents on welfare and almost all of them poor and supposedly living with their children in "disadvantaged" and "culturally deprived" homes, were the victims of yet another and quite vicious Great White Racist Myth.

They were imagined by the middle-class Whites who ran the school system (even including one or two OPD people) to be somehow both incapable of and uninterested in caring adequately for their children and thus unable to help the schools educate those children properly. It was assumed that, because they were poor and African American, they would be parents who were "hard to reach," that they would not want or would not be able to take part in school activities or take on a commanding role in defining what they wanted the schools to do for their children and then to make sure that the schools did what they wanted.

What pernicious nonsense all this turned out to be! Given half a chance to assume some real control over the educational lives of their children and despite the fact that many of our families had two working parents and often only a single parent, almost all these parents (including fathers) at one time or another eagerly stepped in and became genuine partners in running the school and making sure their children got what they deserved. True, we did not have at that time in Roxbury many non-English-speaking parents, so our job was that much easier. But subsequent experiences have taught me that the very same rules apply to all parents, no matter what their native languages or cultures may be. The "parent involvement" problem, in short, lies not in the parents but almost always in the schools.

This new era of parent/professional collaboration in the subsystem, in addition to creating a remarkable esprit de corps on the part of everyone in the schools, also had some interesting practical effects. One of the problems we first encountered at the Boardman, for instance, was that every school—or at least all schools in Roxbury—had orders to keep their doors locked during the school day in order to protect the children from the intrusion of undesirable elements—drug pushers, high school–age hoods, and assorted other possible troublemakers. This rule—and the very real dangers it was intended to guard against—made it difficult to institute and maintain the "open door" policy that both we and the parents wanted. But in consultation with the parents group and with that group's approval we went ahead and unlocked the doors.

Rather than the school being overrun by undesirable elements, what happened was that since the school was always filled with parents either working there or visiting, the parents themselves simply took over the job of policing the school and guaranteeing everyone's safety. Anyone entering the school was immediately either welcomed by the parents or instructed in no uncertain terms to beat a hasty retreat, depending upon the legitimacy of the visitor's business. And the Boardman's doors remained always open.

It was through experiences such as this that the teachers, for their part, began to see the parents as allies, not only as compatriots in the task of educating children, but also as unindicted co-conspirators in their attempt to change and reform the Boston school system. Somehow it began to seem that everyone, all of us, were at last on the same side.

Thus both we school people and the parents themselves learned a lasting lesson: that parents were far from being the problem that most Boston school people thought them to be. Indeed, given the full respect due them as human beings and as the people primarily responsible for the upbringing and education of their children, parents were not the problem at all but an essential part of the solution.

Indeed, what eventually became utterly clear to us thick-headed OPD types was the simple, permanent, unalterable and obvious fact that the children belonged not to the staff at the Boardman, or to the Office of Program Development, or to the Boston Public Schools, or the Commonwealth of Massachusetts, or even the federal government, but to the parents. Since most of us OPD types were ourselves parents of children in the Massachusetts public schools (and mostly not happily so) just how this fact escaped our notice for so long has always remained something of a mystery.

What Went On in Those Classrooms

The type of developmental schooling we were instituting in the subsystem clearly requires all of the previously described attributes—not merely that quite different approach to how a school should be run but a quite different approach to how a classroom should be organized and, indeed, a different approach to everything that happens in that classroom and the school itself during the school day.

To begin with, a fundamental premise of such schooling is the practice of vertical grouping, organizing preschool and kindergarten children together in early childhood classes, first through third graders together in primary classes, and fourth through sixth graders in intermediate classes. With this arrangement, students can move at their own speed, often with older children helping younger children as needed, and no child arbitrarily "held back" or kept from advancing as rapidly as possible by any conventional rigid grade structure.

Another obvious requirement: When we first arrived at the Boardman, the classrooms were filled with row upon row of desks and chairs all screwed to the floor. The educational process conducted there was one that was all too familiar to me—all of the students sitting more or less quietly and attentively at their desks being instructed by the teacher at the front of the room, with all children in the class essentially being "taught" the same lesson at the same time.

So the first thing we had to do was to unscrew and toss out those desks and replace them with movable tables and chairs, with bookshelves and storage cabinets to hold the wealth of learning materials with which each room had to be stocked—all the ESS math and science materials, Cuisenaire rods and Dienes blocks, aquariums and terrariums, gerbil cages, rugs on the floors, art and music materials, and hundreds of books for children to browse through and read and take home with them if they wanted to (the building was too small to have a library), in short, all the things the children would need to conduct their "messing about" activities.

The Boardman's reading program began with everything in those richly stocked primary classrooms being carefully labeled—the door, the chalkboard, the tables, the chairs, the rabbit cage and the rabbit inside it, the fish tank and the fish, the electric typewriter, the teacher's desk, and each child's cubbyhole; everything had a card attached to it with its descriptive word written on the card.

No one (except perhaps other children) ever told a child what those words meant. They had to figure each word out for themselves—or ask another kid. In this exploratory fashion, the children began to acquire and understand the great and fundamental principle of symbolic representation, that those funny-looking squiggles on the cards (and later in the books all around the room) "stand for" the objects to which they are attached (and also to the words in all those books). And that representation does not change—the squiggles making up the noun *chair* almost always referred to that thing with four legs that everyone sits on, no matter what the context might be.

One teacher, Jane Fitzgerald, also instituted Sylvia Ashton Warner's "organic reading" approach. Her children quickly learned that if, in addition to the words written on the labels in the room, they wanted to know how other words looked when written, they could go to their teacher and ask for that word. She would then write the word on a card and give it back to the child. That word then became the child's very own special word—and many of the words they asked for and received were not words normally found in the sanitized vocabulary of basal readers. Each child thus began a collection of his or her very own words. Gradually, as a child's collection of word cards grew larger and larger, the teacher would show that child how his or her words could be arranged into sentences and then sentences that told stories. The stories were then written down by the children and turned into small books (illustrated by the child) and passed around the class for other children to read.

Since the school never used anything like a basal reader or a canned reading series, these child-produced books, along with large quantities of both new and classic children's books, were essentially the "language arts" program of the school. As the output of such books grew, the children began to discover one of the great but almost totally neglected educational inventions of all time—the electric typewriter (and now, of course, the computer). It quickly became apparent that even 6- and 7-year-olds not only were fascinated by the typewriter but also could quite quickly and easily learn to hunt and peck on it and write their stories and books. Every month the stories written by the children were collected and published in book form. Each story included the author's name. These books were studied by the children and used as examples for further taping, reading, and publishing. A few copies were kept in the classroom library, while the remaining copies were taken home to be shared with other family members—especially the proud parents.

Or take two additional examples, Michael and John, two boys in Barbara Jackson's primary class. As Ms. Jackson puts it, "Michael was a boy with many problems—obesity, an overindulgent mother, an only child, and a distinct dislike for reading." In October, when most of the class was studying the voyages of Columbus to America from a history book, Michael suddenly volunteered to copy for classroom display the map that was illustrated in the text. He did a beautiful job, enlarging the map, printing words in appropriate places, and finally coloring it. The map was placed in a prominent position near the classroom door. Michael would beam every time visitors came into the room and made note of his map.

From that point on," says Ms. Jackson,

Michael would search out books with maps he could copy. He would seek help in finding out what kind of a map it was and what the words were on the map. He became our official mapmaker. Eventually in his searching for maps he became interested in other reading matter and soon was on his way to reading books on other subjects. Incidentally, there was a spin-off as a result of Michael's venture into mapmaking. Other children became interested in maps. Atlases were constantly consulted. Children's map-reading skills improved throughout the class.

Ms. Jackson's second example, John, in his 2nd year of school, was virtually a nonreader. He clearly was performing way below his verbal capacities in reading. According to anyone's expectations, John should have been reading—but he wasn't. One Monday during the sharing period, John spoke with great animation about an exciting incident that had happened between his cousin's dog and a German shepherd the previous day. Ms. Jackson, as he talked, quickly made a note of his story on a piece of paper. Later she made a mimeograph master sheet for John to see. Together they read the story over and over again until eventually John could read it verbatim. During the day, John made copies of his story and passed them out to his friends.

Ms. Jackson informed John that she would copy onto masters any other stories he could tell. Then he could have his stories stapled together in book form. She provided him with blank tape for him to record his additional stories. This one incident seemed suddenly to have awakened John to the relationship between the spoken and written word so that reading suddenly had meaning for him. He made rapid progress in reading from then on.

Or to take a quite different example, there was a young man I shall call Larry, a handsome, strapping 12-year-old who often came to school covered with welts that had obviously been inflicted by the buckle of a large belt. Larry lived with his single-parent mother, who believed that the only way to control him was to beat him with a belt for even the slightest infraction of a rule—or sometimes for no reason at all.

The result of this treatment at home, combined with Larry's previous unhappy experiences in Boston's schools, was that at the Boardman Larry was uncontrollable. He could not stand to be touched by anyone, child or adult. If a classmate or a teacher came anywhere near him, Larry would lash out with both fists, causing many a bloody nose and black eye. He was also not about to do anything anyone told him to do, paid no attention in class, asked intrusive questions, daydreamed, and disrupted the entire school—again, a kid who could easily be diagnosed as having Attention Deficit Hyperactivity Disorder and thus a candidate for "special" education of some sort and perhaps even drugged with Ritalin, which we at the Boardman would never have dreamed of suggesting. Many a staff session at the Boardman was spent trying to figure out what to do with and for Larry.

Then one day Larry came to his teacher and said he would like to start a small garden in a box underneath one of the windows at the back of the classroom. He knew, he said, what he wanted to grow and claimed he knew how to manage a garden. The teacher was dubious, but said, fine, go ahead. It might even keep Larry out of trouble.

Several of the teachers in the school thought they were pretty good at growing things, but they quickly realized that with Larry they were in the presence of a genius. Larry could get almost anything to grow—plants, grass, fungi, anything at all. He could grow things in paper cups, in coffee cans, in mud, in sand. He not only grew things but also read everything he could get his hands on about gardening and plants. He become, in short order, the school's savant in plant biology and began teaching his specialty to other children, and especially to children in the primary grades who absolutely adored him as he showed them how to grow things themselves.

So Larry became one of the Boardman's star pupils and assistant teachers, but that was not enough to save him. Although we took his mother to court several times, the beatings did not stop and eventually Larry ended up in the hospital. Finally the courts took him away from his mother—and us— and provided him with residential care at a state institution.

This use of "the real thing" (as in the case of Larry's plants) was one of the cardinal principles of the Boardman's developmental schooling. In Ms. Jackson's class, for instance, one of the sparks was live animals. At one time or another the classroom had gerbils, fish, rabbits, snails, turtles, frogs, ants, and a canary. The study of these creatures included taking care of them, reading about them, writing about them, classifying them, weighing them, and mathematically charting their growth and development.

At one point some of the children wanted to have a fish tank in their room similar to one in another room. Their research on how to proceed involved answers to such questions as what precisely would be needed, what kinds of fish to purchase, how to set up and take care of the tank, and so on. Children who had tanks at home reported on them. A visit to the public library was necessary to obtain books on the subject. A list was composed of the necessary materials to build a tank.

When the tank finally arrived, store milk containers (pints, quarts, gallons) were used to measure the amount of water put into the tank. The terminology *tropical fish* initiated a global study of what *tropical* meant. The temperature of the water was measured daily with a thermometer that was marked off in twos. Counting everything by twos as a base became a big class thing.

Guppies were first placed in the tank. Question: How can we keep the water clean? Answer: "We can balance the aquarium by including snails and water plants." Interested children volunteered to care for the tank and feed the fish. Feeding charts were made. Periodic observations were reported to the class. Stories and pictures were created and displayed around the room.

One story indicated that a female was "pregnant." Soon there were babies to report. The babies did not live long, but their death precipitated questions on fish skeletons and eventually the relationships of all forms of life to each other.

A large dead fish was brought to class. Children, assisted by the teacher, dissected the fish. Using a diagram of a fish found in one of the classroom encyclopedias, the children noted and named the different organs found in the fish's body. Later a large copy of the diagram was made as a permanent record of the activity. The children also compared the bone structure of the fish to the bone structure of a human hand as seen in an X-ray picture one of the boys brought to school.

More connections: The calcium and limestone formed from the skeletons of animals in the water was related to a project on sedimentary rocks. Children recalled that limestone was placed in the tank water with a turtle to keep the turtle's shell hard. Dead fish were used to fertilize the soil when Indians planted corn for the Pilgrims. Calcium in milk keeps people's teeth healthy.

This ongoing "fish project" continued to interest the children throughout the year with the inclusion of different fish species in the tanks and ultimately the study of other forms of marine life. A huge mural of imaginary sea forms was constructed by the children and became the focus of a series of fantasy stories created by the children. By the end of the year three children had received parental permission to have an aquarium at home. A culminating activity for the entire year was an all-day picnic at the seashore during the last week of school where the children got the chance to see marine life in its natural context.

Clearly one rule of developmental schooling at the Boardman was the use of everyday "stuff" brought in by the children and turned into intrinsically interesting learning materials—such as, for instance, that dead fish. These also included such items as:

> Empty milk cartons used as planters or model buildings or simply as containers and measures.
> Playing cards for number games.
> Dice for reading and number games, commercial or childmade.
> Pebbles, rocks, stones for classifying, for numbers, for scientific experiments.
> String for art projects, mobiles, science experiments.
> Dirt, sand for nature study (Larry's botanical projects).
> Pieces of cloth, a sewing kit for art and dramatic play.
> Clothespins for displays and identifying personal belongings.
> Miscellaneous objects such as detergent bottles, rulers, tape measures, a baby scale, tongue depressors, straws, masking and Scotch tape.

A further basic tenet of developmental schooling is that the activities that the students engage in should for the most part be activities that they themselves have generated, always with the guiding assistance of a teacher or some other adult. These could be activities instigated and conducted by a single student—reading a book or painting a picture—or an activity inspired in a group of students by an intrinsically captivating classroom material (the gerbil cage) and by a teacher's skilled wondering (how do those gerbils manage to stay alive anyway?) or an activity thought up jointly by teacher and students and engaged in by the entire class—putting on a play, composing music using the Orff materials, dancing in their eurhythmic classes, or building a dinosaur time line along the school's walls.

But—the students and teachers always have to be free at any time to alter what they are doing to take advantage of and follow up on not only the good but also Duckworth's "wonderful" ideas and especially all the questions that inevitably occur when students are allowed and encouraged to think and learn for themselves. As a general rule, however, if a child is or a group of children are happily and productively engaged in studying something or perhaps just reading a book, they are not to be disturbed until they have finished whatever it is they are doing.

Indeed, as we progressed in the development of this approach, several of the teachers at the Boardman, and especially Ms. Jackson and Ms. Fitzgerald, advanced the startling heresy that, given the kinds of classrooms they were running, all the non–severely disabled children would learn to read and do basic arithmetic by the end of their 3rd year in the school with little if any formal instruction or the use of any formal curriculum at all.

But What About Assessment and Accountability?

Another thing we did throughout the subsystem was to introduce a different "grading and evaluation" system. We did away with grades entirely by simply replacing them with written teacher comments on report cards. This reporting system was one small part of our much larger research and evaluation process that our in-house OPD research group was attempting to design and operate for each school and for the subsystem experiment as a whole.

Since the Boston system—like every system in the country—was required by state law to administer yearly standardized basic skills achievement tests, we decided that we would have to use them as one small part of our evaluation system whether we thought they would really be useful or not.

But our ultimate aim was to develop a student assessment process that covered a broad range (in the first place) of cognitive skills—such as the ability to think clearly, to reason well, and to discover and solve problems. We also wanted to know if the students were beginning to develop their epistemological capacities by exploring the great human question of how do we know what we think we know and whether they were thus developing their innate ability to construct their own knowledge. But we also wanted to track the development of a host of other skills, talents, and attributes—whether our children were displaying previously unnoticed talents in music, the arts, and science; whether they really were developing initiative and responsibility for their own learning; whether they were becoming people who cared about one another; whether they were beginning to see themselves as competent, capable human beings able to think for themselves; whether they were beginning to see the act of inquiring and learning as a satisfying and rewarding experience in and of itself, something they could learn to love, and not simply dreary "school" drudgery, et cetera, et cetera.

We knew we did not have the expertise within the Boston system to develop this kind of an evaluation setup, since our research people were psychometricians primarily adept at conventional IQ and academic achievement testing. So as part of our overall effort to involve Greater Boston's extraordinarily rich array of institutions of higher education, we canvased the local colleges and universities and their schools of education (including Harvard, the Massachusetts Institute of Technology, Boston College, and Boston University) to see if we could not form a working partnership with academic cognitive and developmental psychologists to help us design and try out such a new system—as well as coming in and working with us in our attempts to establish and practice developmental schooling.

In my continuing naïveté about the people and institutions of higher education despite my experiences at ESI, I still believed that it should be possible—indeed, that it should be intellectually, socially, and morally obvious and necessary—that the colleges and universities and particularly the schools of education throughout the Boston area would be vitally interested in helping and eager to become involved with the large and deeply troubled urban school system right at their front doors. Many of the academics in those institutions had for years been loudly and publicly condemning the people who ran and taught in the Boston system as being reactionary racists and educational dinosaurs, so of course they would do everything in their power to come in and help a promising piece of that school system that was attempting to bring about significant change.

Over and over again we pleaded with the people we knew in those institutions to join and help us, and we actually received considerable help from Theodore Sizer, who was then dean of the Harvard Graduate School of Education, in getting OPD started, as well as the continued support of the people at his institution. But in general, while some of these university people and their institutions expressed interest, there seemed to be simply no way that their organizational structure would allow them to commit their own time and resources to such an arrangement. Although we did work out some joint summer programs (paid for by us at OPD), when fall came the higher education faculty people always had to return to their primary tasks of teaching and research at their own institutions, leaving us on our own. If we wanted to get more help, we essentially would have had to hire the institutions and their people.

But we didn't have the money to do that, in addition to the fact that we were not all that eager to pay for something we thought those institutions of higher education should be brimming with eagerness to do and pay for on their own. This would be part of the job of fulfilling Benjamin Franklin's vision of what an American university should be when he founded the University of Pennsylvania—an institution dedicated to the improvement of human welfare equally through teaching, research, *and community service.*

So, in part because of this major higher education flaw, we at OPD had to make it—or fail to make it—on our own. In the case of our research-and-evaluation crew, we pretty much had to make do with conventional psychometrics while we worked in house on more profoundly developmental assessment measures.

All our students were given group IQ tests, and many were also given individual IQ tests. This told us that our "disadvantaged," "culturally deprived" African American children, especially when given individual IQ tests by an African American tester, exhibited the full range of a perfectly normal population, at least in those limited IQ terms.

All our children also, of course, had to be given those systemwide, state-ordered standardized basic skills achievement tests, and the results there were also no surprise. Many of our older students—those who remained from the previous Boardman population as well as those who had come to us from other Boston schools—scored poorly on those tests, often several "grade levels" below what their IQ scores suggested they should be achieving. This led us to suspect that it might just be the traditional schools and the type of schooling they had received in those schools that might possibly account for some of the discrepancy—or what later came to be called the "achievement gap"—between our "disadvantaged poor and minority" children and middle class, nonminority children.

But even though we were not overly impressed by or interested in conventional academic test score results anyway, we were compelled by those state laws to use them. So we established our own approach to their use, an approach that has since come to be called the "value-added" approach to testing. We threw out the notion of saying how many of our children were at or not at "grade level" and said instead that the only thing we were interested in was whether on any particular test—and especially the reading and math skills tests—a student demonstrated at the very least a year's progress in a year's time, as measured by that particular test.

Thus, if a student who would conventionally be a fourth-grade reader but tested at a second-grade level moved from that second-grade level to at least a third-grade level during the year (and if possible, to a fourth-grade level or above), then that child was succeeding—*and so was the school.* As it turned out, almost all our students met those minimum standards of a year's growth in a year's time. And of course, there was no way, given our organic, unpredictable, unpredetermined curriculum, that standardized tests in the conventional subject matter compartments could possibly make any sense. So we never bothered to give them. And that was as far as we were willing to go with standardized testing.

None of this meant that we were uninterested in whether our children might be learning the "content" of the conventional academic subjects, the particular (and small) range of things that the academic curricular "experts" had selected from the vast storehouse of human knowledge and decided that students should learn and be tested on. It was simply that we believed we were quite capable of deciding whether what the children were learning as a result of their developmental schooling was intellectually and culturally worthy, even if much of that learning embraced many things that were not in the curriculum guides or on the tests, very much including Eleanor Duckworth's "wonderful" ideas.

And at the High School . . .

Meanwhile, events of a different kind were taking place at one of the subsystem's other schools—the small high school we had started in one end of the Lewis Junior High building that also housed our experimental junior high. When the high school started in September 1966, it consisted of 150 volunteer African American students in "Grades" 9 and 10, recruited as volunteers from surrounding Boston junior high and high schools, and a handful of OPD's volunteer teachers. It was run by two veteran White high school teachers (and two extraordinary women), Grace Whitaker and Teresa Hamrock. While a woman was allowed to be headmaster (*sic*) of the all-female Girls Latin High School and Ms. Hamrock had been head of a school called Girls High School, these two subsystem women were the only women in the system allowed to run a coed high school. (At Girls High, a school for young women who were deemed not qualified for anything but largely vocational courses, one of the courses was something called "power stitching," which out in the real world paid $1.25 an hour. This was a time when these young women could make $50 a trick if they chose to be self-employed in the city's Combat Zone.)

At the beginning of that 1966 school year, both the staff and the students (a bunch of real tough, turned-off, African American male and female ghetto kids) were wary of one another and felt their way hesitantly toward some kind of working relationship. For instance, the students were involved in the planning of a completely interdisciplinary curriculum. They created peer group seminars, they participated in the selection of classroom materials, they made their own films with a local African American filmmaker, they studied Black history, and they listened to local (and militant) Black civil rights speakers whom they themselves selected and invited. So by the spring of 1968, the staff had made a good many departures from the traditional ways of running a high school, and the students were beginning to warm up to the school.

For instance, the teachers in consultation with the students developed a wildly successful (as measured by student fascination and involvement) interdisciplinary course called Heroes, combining art, English, and social studies in a study of what heroes are and are not. The students studied the heroes of two films—the Gary Cooper character in *High Noon* (some of the boys in the class thought Cooper was out of his mind to behave the way he did) and the Sidney Poitier character in *A Raisin in the Sun*—combined with a study of the Sumerian Epic of Gilgamesh and of the Trojan War (this was a big hit) and a comparison of *West Side Story* and *Romeo and Juliet*, which introduced the question of heroism and nonheroism in their own gangs.

Slowly, even the "bandits," as the staff called them, the really tough, turned-off cases, both male and female, began to respond to what was happening.

Then came Thursday, April 4, 1968. When the news struck that Martin Luther King Jr. had been assassinated that night, no one on the school staff had any idea what might happen when school opened the following day. The teachers all appeared at school that following morning expecting riots at the very least.

Surprisingly, most of the students showed up as well. They, like the entire Roxbury community, were angry, scared, and very "uptight." It was during this period that handbills were being distributed throughout the African American community warning residents to "cool it!" and claiming that the White Boston police force might launch an armed attack on all Blacks in the city. All electricity, gas, and water, said the handbills, would be turned off in Roxbury, and no food would be available unless Black people stocked up enough to last for 30 days. Guns and ammunition should also be stockpiled, the populace was warned, but only for the defense of African American homes (the slogan was "Defensive Now, Offensive Later").

In this atmosphere of high tension, then, the students and staff confronted each other on the morning of April 5. It quickly became apparent to the staff that a small group of the "bandits" were suddenly emerging as the leadership of the student body, although none of them had been elected to any formal student government. In particular, one of the boys, a rangy, handsome Black Muslim named Steven Green, who had a pronounced stammer, took over as chief of the governing junta.

The first thing the students, led by Steve and the bandit junta, did was to ask for a moratorium on all classes for the day and the convening of a student assembly run by and for themselves alone to decide what they wanted to do—with no participation by the staff. Ms. Whitaker and Ms. Hamrock immediately bought into that proposal. The students spent that entire Friday arguing among themselves draw up a list of demands.

When school reopened on Monday morning, the bandit junta and an elected student representative from each of the school's classrooms appeared and announced that this 22-member group now constituted the official student board of the school. Two days later they presented Ms. Whitaker and Ms. Hamrock with their list of demands, which they had typed up and run off on the school's ditto machine.

The list contained 15 items, falling roughly into two groups. The first group revolved around a desire for many of the regular rituals that go with traditional high schooling—a more elaborate graduation ceremony for the ninth grade, a semiformal dance, a class day for the ninth grade, a class picture, and "A SYMBOL TO IDENTY OURSELVES AND WHAT WE STAND FOR" (neither spelling nor typing was among these students' major educational achievements to that date. Indeed, a few of them were still reading at a third-grade level).

The second group of demands was aimed at establishing the fact that they were autonomous human beings and had a right to exert some control over their own destiny in school. They did not wish to be treated as incompetent juveniles.

The list of demands called for some small adjustments in the school rules and ended with this major demand: "BEFOR A STUDENT CAN BE SUSPENDED HE OR SHE MUST BE DESIDED BY THE BOARD. WHEN A STUDENT COMES BACK THEY MUST ACCOMPLIED BY A PARENTS. A BOARD MEMBER MUST BE PRESENT." One intent of this demand was immediately clear—the students wanted a piece of the administrative action that galled them most acutely: the power of the school staff to remove them from school for a day or 2 on those rare occasions when the administrators could find no other method of dealing with student obstreperousness.

But that was not all. A persistent problem at the school had been the reaction of some parents to their child being suspended for a day or two (on those few instances when this was deemed to be necessary). In some cases, this had led to heated confrontations between the school staff and parents, who thought their children were being unjustly treated. What Steve and the other students wanted, they explained later, was, yes, some say over why people should or should not be suspended but also a chance to make it clear to parents that a suspension was not an arbitrary, ruthless act on the part of the staff. The reason for having a board member present when the parents brought a student back was to protect the staff. It would be up to the board member to explain why both the staff and the students had decided that a suspension was necessary.

Mss. Whittaker and Hamrock and the rest of the staff accepted the establishment of the student board and all the proposed new school rules, with one exception, the request that "we would like to name the school the COLETTA KING HIGH SCHOOL." The staff had to explain that only the Boston School Committee had the legal power to name schools.

But Not Just the Students

But in addition to what I believed to be the subsystem successes with the students and their parents, I was equally delighted by the changes that were occurring in the teachers and administrators at all the subsystem's schools. What increasingly enchanted the teachers most, they said, was the intellectual energy the students displayed whenever they were not just allowed but actually encouraged to cut loose and think and learn for themselves, to have and pay attention to their own ideas (à la Eleanor Duckworth). The teachers could not help admiring the intellectual independence and self-reliance the students exhibited when challenged to think for themselves rather than simply feeding back to the teachers whatever it was that the curriculum guides said they should be learning.

Gradually, these experiences at the Boardman and at the junior and senior high schools led all of us at OPD to make the, to us, startling but, when we thought about it, perfectly obvious discovery that there was no intrinsic, no necessary, connection between any child's achievement levels as tested by the standardized tests and that child's intelligence, the child's ability to think and use his or her mind.

This hardly meant that such "basic" reading and math skills were useless or that they could not and did not make a significant contribution to any child's intellectual, social, and moral development. But we slowly became convinced—as I had been with the social studies program—that traditional schooling had things exactly backward. Instead of assuming that the primary job of school was to teach children and young people their "basic" skills so that they could thereby learn to use their minds, we began to believe that the job was first to allow, encourage, and challenge children to think, to be intellectual explorers, to learn to love learning. Only then, we believed, could we convince the students that acquiring the ability to read and write well in order to express what they thought, to continue to think well and clearly, and to learn more about the things they were interested in learning was a worthwhile enterprise.

All these great, if hardly new, discoveries, I am convinced, both stemmed from and were responsible for the fact that the teachers were radically changing their ideas about what "teaching" should be. Instead of standing in front of a group of bored and inevitably hostile students and attempting to instruct them in all those skills and all that knowledge that the curriculum mandates and the textbooks said they should learn, the teachers now found themselves becoming guides and advisors to students who were making decisions and learning essentially on their own. It was more like coaching football than what they had always conceived classroom teaching to be. And to their continuing amazement and delight, the students were no longer bored and hostile (or at least most of them weren't).

Approaching a Small Miracle

But history was rapidly catching up with us at the Boardman. After only 2½ years of the subsystem experiment, the moment approached when the decrepit Boardman building finally had to be torn down and the children moved into a spanking new, much larger school building a few blocks away. And it was then that we at OPD began to feel that perhaps our experiment, at least insofar as the parents and the African American community were concerned, might actually be a success.

The Boardman parents were immediately concerned (as were we at OPD) about what would happen to the 220-student subsystem early childhood and elementary programs if they became only one part of a much larger, 700-student school operation. In the collaborative discussions that followed between OPD and the elected leaders of the parents group, the parents came up with the idea that the subsystem should take over the entire new school, which had been tentatively designated to become the Joseph Lee School, named after a prominent White Boston philanthropist and the father of a longtime School Committee member.

Although some of us at OPD worried that a 700-student school was simply too large for a developmental program such as the Boardman's (200 being just about the right size, we thought), the parents group as a whole eagerly adopted the takeover idea and then, with the strong support of the African American civil rights leadership and OPD, took the matter several steps further.

The parents, of course, were fully aware that, because of a racial-balance law that had been passed in 1970 by the state legislature, the new school would have to be racially integrated and that therefore 350 of the school's 700 seats would have to be reserved for White students. They knew as well that there was no way that White parents in the city could or should be forced to have their children assigned to the school. They wanted no part of any such arbitrary, tyrannical disaster for White parents any more than they wanted it for African American parents in the system. They were true believers in the subsystem's basic rule that all the parents and students in a subsystem school (or any public school, for that matter) must be volunteers, there by choice, not compulsion.

They knew, too, that since there was a substantial waiting list of African American parents who wanted their children admitted to the Boardman, they would have no difficulty recruiting the necessary 150 such students to fill the school's "Black" quota. The problem was how to recruit the parents of 350 White children and persuade them voluntarily to enroll their children in the school. Their answer was that they would go out to White schools throughout the city and meet with parents, extol the virtues of the Boardman program, and persuade them to send their children to the school.

We OPD types understood all too well the enormous courage such a proposal demanded on the part of a group of perfectly ordinary African American parents who were not accustomed to confronting the organized bastions
of White society at a time when many of those White neighborhoods were
seething with anger over the state and federal pressure to desegregate the
schools. We were not at all sure that if we had been in their position we would
have been able to summon such courage.

The first thing we at OPD did was to sit down with Superintendent Bill
Ohrenberger and the internal leadership of the system to discuss the possibility of voluntarily integrating the new school, presenting it not just as a way to
get the new school opened but also as the foundation for a plan to comply
with the state's orders to racially balance the entire system (and to meet what
we knew full well would eventually be a federal court order to integrate the
schools).

Ohrenberger and the city were already launched on a massive school-
building program—the program we at the OPD Educational Planning Center were responsible for programming and designing. Our involvement meant
that this building program guaranteed many future opportunities to repeat a
successful experiment at the new school, including the reverse arrangement
in which African American parents would be voluntarily recruited for the new
schools in White areas.

But in addition to the opportunity presented by new schools, we also
proposed that existing neighborhood schools might be converted into such
schools of parent and teacher/administrator choice. Within something like
10 years, we speculated, the entire school system could be peacefully desegregated through this process of making every school a voluntary "magnet" school
and thus without any "forced" busing.

Ohrenberger immediately applauded the idea, seeing it as possibly the
perfect way for the system and the city to defuse the racial bomb that the School
Committee was building throughout the city's White communities. So he
authorized OPD to continue working quietly with the Boardman parents and
the leadership of the African American community to come up with a workable plan for the new school that could be brought before an unsuspecting
School Committee.

What the Boardman parent leadership and the leaders of the African
American civil rights groups eventually did was to march themselves downtown to a meeting with the five all-White members of the Boston School
Committee. They officially requested—although they made it clear that this
was not just a request but essentially a demand on the part of the whole African American community—that the subsystem program become the program
of the entire new school and that the school be named after Boston's famed
19th-century African American journalist William Monroe Trotter.

They also insisted that the School Committee reaffirm its original commitment to the subsystem parents that, once a child was admitted to kindergarten or any other grade at the Trotter, that child was guaranteed a seat in the subsystem's two other schools, the Lewis Junior High and the Pierce High School (these two schools were later moved and became magnet schools, the Phillis Wheatley Middle School and Copley Square High School, now the Muriel Snowden School for International Studies).

In return, said the Boardman parents, they would go out and attempt to recruit enough White parents and students from all over the city to make up half the new school's enrollment, an effort assisted by the fact that their crumbling, dilapidated school had in the course of its 3-year existence ceased to be the "worst" school in Boston and, as a result of newspaper coverage and word of mouth, had become the single most renowned and admired elementary school in the city. Indeed, White parents from other parts of the city had often tried to get their children admitted to the all–African American Boardman but had been turned down by OPD because there was already a long waiting list of African American children from the school's nearby neighborhoods, who had first call if a seat became available.

To everyone's surprise, the School Committee agreed to all the demands of the Boardman parents, although most members of the committee and the school system's hierarchy privately expressed profound doubts about whether the Boardman parents could actually persuade White parents to choose voluntarily to put their children—especially their kindergarten and primary-grade children—on buses and send them into the "Dangerous Black Ghetto" to go to school. The committee even agreed that if by some miracle any suburban White parents wanted to volunteer their children for the new school, that would be okay too—but they would have to provide their own transportation.

Superintendent Ohrenberger, however, was overjoyed at this development. He proceeded to persuade the School Committee to officially order OPD and the school system to prepare a brochure describing the wonders of the new school and its subsystem program. He ordered as well that the brochure come from him as superintendent (with his picture on page 1) and that it immediately be distributed to all White public school parents in the city. When the brochure went out, it did not contain a guarantee that free bus transportation would be provided, because the state refused to put up the money. All it could say was that the school system hoped that such transportation would become available. But initially White parents thought they might have to carpool their children to the school.

Most of the members of the White hierarchy of the school system—and, for that matter, most of the White population of the city and many members of the African American community—thought this a harebrained scheme if ever there was one, given the fact that the city's civil rights and desegregation struggle was reaching a fever pitch at this particular moment, with angry African American and White activists staging rallies and picketing the School Committee headquarters.

In recent months, in part as a result of the assassination of Martin Luther King Jr., the African American community had actually been preparing for an armed attack by the White power structure. Given this situation, why would any sensible White parent take a chance on sending his or her children into what everyone thought could be a very dangerous and possibly explosive situation in the African American community?

But the Boardman parents stuck to their revolutionary agenda. With OPD help, pairs of parents went out to PTA meetings in the White parts of the city, including hotbeds of antidesegregation activity such as South Boston and Charlestown. We at OPD fielded responses to the brochure that had been sent out, most respondents asking further questions about the new Trotter program and a few actually signing their children up, even though we could not guarantee that the state would provide their children with free bus transportation. Eventually the state did come through with such transportation, which began to make the entire enterprise appear to be a bit more possible.

As the summer of 1969 progressed, we at OPD began the staggering task of recruiting additional teachers and planning for more than a doubling of the Boardman's enrollment, not necessarily expecting that the parents and we could pull the whole thing off. What we slowly began to realize—and even hope for—was that if the Boardman parents and the Black community leaders, with some OPD assistance, could actually succeed in voluntarily integrating the brand new William Monroe Trotter School, the school would become one of the country's first magnet schools, a school designed to attract voluntarily both minority and nonminority parents and students with the aim of peacefully desegregating Boston's schools—and perhaps, later, all the nation's schools.

By the end of the summer, the parents of more than 350 White children had actually signed their children up to attend the school, including some 20 children of suburban parents mainly from nearby Brookline who were not supplied with free bus transportation as the Boston parents were. But could anyone really expect that a miracle might happen, that when the moment of truth came and those White Boston parents had to put their children on their buses they would actually do so?

In addition to this uncertainty, we also had to face the fact that this idea of making the Trotter a magnet school was not universally applauded in the African American civil rights community. Indeed, a few of the Black civil rights activists opposed the plan. They felt that the first new school built in Roxbury in the past 30 years should serve only African American children, whose education had for years been so unjustly neglected, even if that meant that the school would be a segregated school.

So when the great moment arrived when the Boston schools were to open on that cool September morning in 1969, there was a large, buzzing crowd gathered on the street outside the Trotter. A significant part of that crowd was made up of unhappy activists, some of them jeering at the African American teachers and the African American parents who were bringing their children to school—the crowd calling them "Uncle Toms" and "Aunt Sadies."

But when the yellow buses and the parental carpools containing the suburban students rolled up and to the amazement of all onlookers actually unloaded 350 White students, the hecklers were stunned into silence, and the crowd quickly dispersed. A small miracle had actually happened.

What That Small Miracle Meant

When those 350 White children got off their buses and cars to attend the Trotter, neither we nor anyone else observing that spectacle could deny that those children were there because their parents wanted them to be there, because those parents had been given a choice. They could have kept their children securely in their neighborhood—and most likely all-White—schools in South Boston, Charlestown, or West Roxbury, including in the case of the suburban parents in their suburban schools and in some of the Boston cases, their largely White parochial schools. But they didn't. They chose instead to put them on those buses and send them halfway across the city into a part of town that everyone in their neighborhoods must have been telling them was dangerous. All this just so that their children could attend some weird, crazy school inhabited solely by African American children, a school where, so the rumors went (and they were true), kindergarten children took off their shoes and danced?

There were other things about the Trotter experience that didn't make much sense to many people. For instance, there was that prediction that White parents might send their older children to the Trotter, but they would never put their kindergarten and primary-grade children on buses. A few days after the Trotter's opening, when the official student count was taken, it turned out that the school opened almost exactly half African American and half White. There was a slight African American imbalance in the upper grades. The kindergarten and primary grades, however, were perfectly balanced, which meant that the White parents were *least* reluctant to put their younger children on buses and send them into the "Black Ghetto."

There was also the fact that, for the most part, the White children were not from the more affluent and presumably more "liberal" sections of Boston (such as Beacon Hill or the Back Bay) but from those supposedly "racist" White, working-class strongholds of South Boston, Charlestown, and Jamaica Plain.

As the first year at the Trotter progressed, those attendance figures shifted slightly, producing a perfectly balanced school at all levels. One of the adjustments that had to be made was the admission of additional White students to make up for 20 or so White suburban children who had to withdraw. The state refused to pay for any interdistrict bus transportation, and those suburban parents, unfortunately, found that the logistical problems of maintaining private carpools for their children rapidly became insurmountable.

So what was it that made all those White parents choose the Trotter? When we asked them why (informally, since, stupidly, neither we at OPD nor any of the educational researchers at the local colleges and universities saw fit to do a formal study of the matter), they said essentially that they came because they had a choice, because they had heard from the Boardman parents and had read in the press that this was a most unusual and exciting school. Which, they said, their neighborhood school definitely was not. Did they know what "open" or "developmental" schooling was? Not really, they said, but from what they heard the children at the Boardman were eager to go to school every day—which, again, was not the case with children at their neighborhood schools. Would they have come, we asked, if their children had been assigned to the Trotter by the school people downtown, without the parents being asked whether they wanted their children to go to this kind of school? Most of them said simply, "No way!" They came, they said, at least in part simply because they had a choice, because they could decide whether this—or any other—was the kind of schooling they wanted for their children.

The African American parents were in roughly the same position. The Boardman parents, of course, were very much there because they wanted their children in the school—after all, they had fought for that right. But the parents of the additional 150 African American students admitted to make up the full complement of 350 "non-White" students gave the same two basic reasons as the White parents. They were attracted by what they'd heard about the school's program or they were essentially escaping from a neighborhood school they didn't like—or both. And they were also there because they had been given a choice.

Were these three subsystem schools absolutely perfect or wonderful schools? Not on your life. There were all sorts of problems in all three schools, including staff members who didn't work out at all and had to be returned to their regular schools.

We also had continual problems maintaining our curricular and fiscal autonomy from the main system downtown, and we always suffered from the fact that we were still operating within a system that was de facto segregated and therefore under constant and deserved attack from civil rights groups and the courts. Nor were the staffs at our three schools immune to the recurring doubts and terrors that would understandably assail any group of people who found themselves voyaging off into uncharted and therefore frightening educational waters.

With (for me) distressing frequency, I would be asked in staff meetings if "they" really wanted us to be trying these strange new ways of teaching children, ways that no one in the Boston system thought could possibly work or be the right way to educate students. I would then ask who "they" were, although we all knew perfectly well that "they" were the higher-ups at school headquarters downtown. So every once in a while I would ask Bill Ohrenberger to make a ceremonial appearance, which he never failed to do, to reassure all of us that we were doing exactly what he wanted us to do.

Regardless of all these normal problems with trying anything innovative in any American public school system, we at OPD took our small miracle at the Trotter and what we saw as the continuing progress at the other subsystem schools to mean that it might actually be possible, given the right circumstances and the necessary local, state, and national political and educational will, progressively to revitalize and even desegregate a typical urban school system and therefore, just possibly, begin to create a new, more just, and truly democratic American system of public schooling.

But that was not to be. In short order the three racist, recalcitrant Boston School Committee members discovered that Ohrenberger intended to obey the law and desegregate the system, so they refused to renew his contract, which also meant that I had to leave the directorship of OPD. OPD, the subsystem, and the Educational Planning Center struggled along for a while, but they were eventually caught up in the city's volatile desegregation crisis and died a slow death.

Despite frantic efforts by what remained of the Educational Planning Center and a few of us who were still deeply concerned but were now forced to operate outside the system, any and all such efforts to implement the choice-based desegregation plan pioneered by the Trotter were ignored by the federal court and its desegregation planners. When the final Boston desegregation plan was ordered in 1975, the three subsystem schools were officially designated as magnets, but only as one part of an essentially "forced busing" plan that had produced the riots outside South Boston High School and massive resistance by segments of the White community. This was followed by White flight to the suburbs, which created in Boston a system that from then on would be predominantly minority and thus impossible to truly integrate. And over the next few years, OPD itself gradually disappeared as the Boston system fell back into being a conventional American school system, essentially the very system that I had endured as a student in Washington and Hartford, the one I had observed not only in Boston but all across the country.

But here I think we need to backtrack for a moment and try to understand how that typical American school system came to be, precisely what its present condition is, and what if anything can be done about it, a task that requires a brief and all-too-sketchy historical exploration.

Chapter 4

The Creation of Two Incompatible Educational Processes

When formal schooling was first widely introduced in both this country and in England in the late 18th and early 19th centuries, simple basic literacy in words and numbers was considered adequate for the nonelite children of the population. Thomas Jefferson, for instance, when he proposed his early version of universal, publicly supported education for Virginia in the late 18th century, called for every one of Virginia's 20 counties to establish schools to which every (White) citizen could send his or her (male) children free for 3 years to be taught the "basic" skills of reading, writing, and arithmetic. Girls would be educated at home, if at all.

Once that minimal amount of practical, down-to-earth schooling was accomplished for all those White males, Jefferson then proposed, each of those schools would select one "boy of best genius" whose parents were too poor to pay for any further education. This boy would be "raked from the rubbish" and be sent free to each county's tuition requiring grammar school. Here those incipient scholars would not be taught everyday practical skills and knowledge but the classical curriculum of Greek, Latin, geography, and "the higher branches of numerical arithmetic"—essentially Darwin's grammar school curriculum.[14]

Indeed, the school experiences of boys on each side of the Atlantic were roughly similar. Alfred Russel Wallace, who independently created the theory of evolution by natural selection, describes his English school experiences in the early 1800s:

> Flogging with a cane was not uncommon for more serious offences, while for slighter ones [the headmaster] would box the ears pretty severely. . . . Caning was performed in the usual old-fashioned way by laying the boy across the desk, his hands being held on one side and his feet on the other, while the master, pulling the boy's trousers tight with one hand, laid on the cane with great vigour with the other. [The headmaster] always caned the boys himself, but the other

masters administered minor punishments, such as slight ear boxes, slapping the palm with a flat ruler, or rapping the knuckles with a round one. . . . A stupid boy, or one who had a bad verbal memory, was often punished for what was called invincible idleness when it was really a congenital incapacity to learn what he took no interest in or what often had no meaning for him. . . .

Next to Latin grammar the most painful subject I learned was geography, which ought to have been the most interesting. It consisted almost entirely in learning by heart the names of the chief towns, rivers and mountains of the various countries from, I think, Pinnock's "School Geography," which gave the minimum of useful or interesting information. It was something like learning the multiplication tables both in the painfulness of the process and the permanence of the results. The incessant grinding in both, week after week, and year after year, resulted in my knowing both the product of any two numbers up to twelve, and the chief towns of any English county so thoroughly, that the result was automatic, and the name of Staffordshire brought into my memory Stafford, Litchfield, Leek, as surely and rapidly as eight times seven brought fifty-six. The labour and mental effort to one who like myself had little verbal memory was very painful, and though the result has been a somewhat useful acquisition during life, I cannot think but that the same amount of mental exertion wisely directed might have produced far greater and more generally useful results. . . . No interesting facts were ever given in connection with these names, no accounts of the country by travelers were ever read, no good maps were ever given us, nothing but the horrid stream of unintelligible place names, to be learned in their due order as belonging to a certain country.

History was very little better, being largely a matter of learning by heart names and dates, and reading the very baldest account of the doings of kings and queens, of wars, rebellions and conquests. Whatever little knowledge of history I have ever acquired has been derived more from Shakespeare's plays and good historical novels than from anything I learned in school.[15]

In Jefferson's American scheme, at the end of 6 years' instruction in the grammar schools, one half of those charity students

are to be discontinued (from among whom the grammar schools will probably be supplied with future masters); and the other half, who are to be chosen for the superiority of their parts and disposition, are to be sent and continued three years in the study of such sciences as they shall choose at William and Mary College.[16]

The sons of the rich during all this time would, of course, be going to the 3-year primary schools, the grammar schools, and William and Mary (and later Jefferson's own University of Virginia) without running any academic gauntlet or being "raked from the rubbish" or experiencing any danger of being "discontinued" for purely financial reasons.

Thus the vast majority of children in this country, including virtually all women and all African Americans, slave or free, were left to learn all their useful practical skills out in the great contextual university of home, farm, and factory, where everyone assumed that the task of conducting such education was quite properly the responsibility of those who ran the homes, farms, and factories.

This in-context apprentice/mentoring educational system as it was practiced in Colonial America has been described by Robert Tarule in his book *The Artisan of Ipswich.* In New England, as in England, he says, formal apprenticeship began (for boys only, of course) at 14, roughly the age of puberty, when the apprentice moved into the household of his master, and lasted until 20 or 21.

> The master was contractually bound to teach the young man to read and write, and do math (at least enough to keep accounts) and to instruct the youth in Christian virtues. The public school, if the town had one, was mostly for children of the elite. Artisans were schooled at home, albeit someone else's. By the age of twenty one, a young man had completed his apprenticeship and become a journeyman, which meant he could work for another master for wages. An apprentice was not paid but received room, board and clothing. At the end, the master typically gave him a suit of clothes and a set of tools. A young artisan married only when he had become a journeyman or, if he was a farmer, after he had acquired enough land to farm.

In his master's household, Tarule continues, an apprentice also learned the "mysteries" of the trade: "his master's physical habits, how to hold a tool, how to put his body behind it. He also learned mental habits; the sequence of work, how one visualized the object, consistent measuring and marking. Once learned, these "habits of workmanship" were used by the artisan throughout his working career.[17]

We must be very careful here to keep straight in our heads what began to happen when in the late 18th and 19th centuries we in this country were beginning to establish our system of universal, tax-supported public schooling. On the one hand, we have to remember what has these days become a familiar refrain: that this country's economic life was becoming more complex and more dependent upon complicated technology and therefore at least appeared to require more highly skilled and better-educated workers.

In the 19th-century world of the Industrial Revolution and especially as agriculture became increasingly mechanized and vastly more productive, huge numbers of workers were either able to or in many cases were forced to abandon agricultural life on the family farm and migrate to work in the factories and offices springing up in the burgeoning cities. Economic success in this new urban environment meant acquiring a set of habits and skills quite different from those required on the farm and in the villages where Tarule's artisans lived, including such simple things as buying food at a store rather than producing it oneself.

There was also the host of new inventions that radically changed the business office—the typewriter instead of the quill pen, along with the new calculating machines and the telephone, all of which suddenly made office work available for women and brought them into that part of the workforce. It also required both men and women to learn to use the industrial world's new technological gadgetry, involving, for example, replacing the spinning wheel and hand loom with water- and electrically-powered, precisely tooled factory machines. There was thus a growing demand for that technically "better educated" but still completely docile workforce.

It was not merely the titans of business and industry but the elite leaders of society in general who were eager for the development of some social mechanism that would turn the hordes of tattered immigrants pouring off the boats (including my own Irish paternal great-grandfather) into well-behaved, hardworking, English-speaking workers and taxpaying citizens. And, of course, those businesspeople and industrialists were not simply happy but eager to turn the job of training future workers over to an educational institution that would be supported not by them but by the public tax system.

On the other hand, these were also the early and middle years of the introduction into this country of all the horrors that were visited upon human beings and especially on children in the European—and in particular the British—factories, mills, and mines. Although serfdom had been technically abandoned in most Western countries, what had been agricultural serfdom was now, in fact, being replaced by an industrial servitude that was not all that different from classical slavery.

The example of Lowell, Massachusetts, one of the birthplaces of the American Industrial Revolution, is instructive here. Lowell was a brand new, carefully and completely designed city founded from scratch in the 1820s by enlightened Boston businessmen as this country's first planned industrial community. Modeled to some extent on the social and economic reforms instituted by the progressive capitalist Robert Owen in New Lanarck in Scotland, Lowell was specifically designed to avoid all of the horrors its planners had seen in the dark satanic mills and vicious slums of Manchester and other English industrial hells. The planners built clean, well-lit, and technologically advanced water-powered textile mills within an almost utopian society for the relatively well-paid young New England farmwomen (the famous Lowell mill girls) they recruited to woman the mills. They built closely supervised boardinghouses and created a host of cultural and educational opportunities for the young women and encouraged them to become schooled and culturally learned.

This comparative utopia lasted only for a decade or 2 until the waves of early 19th-century immigrants, mainly Irish, were brought from Boston to Lowell to dig the Middlesex Canal. They ended up in desperate need of work and were forced to accept the near-starvation wages then being offered by the subsequent, post-utopian mill owners. Immigrant children found themselves chained to the looms for 10 hours a day, 6 days a week, just to keep themselves and their families alive.

Although neither the New Lanark nor the Lowell utopias survived, the altruistic impulses that sparked those experiments showed that it was not just the desire to have a better educated, more industrially productive populace that fueled the creation of universal public schooling in this country. Such schooling was also the result of the simple human need to care properly for the young of the species, in this case the simple desire to rescue this country's children from the brutal slavery of the mills, the mines, and even the many farms where children toiled unceasingly from dawn to dusk.

As all these changes proceeded they began to constitute a profound shift in the Western perception of childhood and the role of children in the economy of the West. Up until this era, most children—all those of the nonaristocratic working classes—had always been looked upon as economically desirable and even necessary. Family farms could not have existed without the labor of farm children. No matter how brutalized children may have been in the mills, mines, and factories, the income provided by their labor in those arenas was in many cases what kept their families from starvation.

As children were increasingly rescued from the endless labor of agricultural and industrial servitude, however, they gradually became not an economic necessity producing family income, but an economic burden consuming that income. In short, the bulk of upper-, middle-, and even working-class children and young people were gradually beginning to assume the role they now largely inhabit—a role in which they make little and often no contribution to the economic survival of their family or their society but rather are a drain on the family finances and an enormous economic burden on society, as well as a rich new market to be eagerly exploited by alert capitalistic entrepreneurs.

Although even today many children of the working poor and especially children of many immigrant families still work to contribute to family income, childhood and adolescents during this period became largely disconnected from the real world of work. Almost all adolescents began to spend an increasing number of years in the world of formal academic schooling, culminating in the present era, when, beyond the mandated time spent in school, large amounts of young people's nonschool time is spent in the separate world of "teen" culture and the mass-media fantasy world of television, the Internet, computer games, and popular music. Many of these young people still work part time, but often primarily for the purpose of supporting their own teen lifestyle rather than helping to support their families.

Learning to Work in School

As a result of this general move over the past 150 or so years to free children from the everyday world of work and put them into the relatively safe if not always humane institution of formal schooling, children and young people would now spend an increasingly large part of their formative years within the four walls of a public school acquiring their "basic academic skills" and some rudimentary vocational skills along with their accompanying docilities of mind and behavior. Since rigid teaching and corporal punishment were part of the standard educational repertoire, many of these schools were most likely only slightly more humane than the factories, mills, and mines from which the children were being rescued, as Alfred Wallace's description of his schooling demonstrates.

In order to pay for this new additional system of expanded schooling, the public would now be taxed to supply semitrained workers for the worlds of business and industry and thereby greatly increase the profits of the owners of those businesses and industries. William Maxwell, the superintendent of the New York City Schools in 1914, put this in words that have a familiar contemporary ring. To solve this problem of how to produce cheap skilled labor, he wrote:

> the exit was obvious—persuade the state to assume the burden. And as a first step to secure their ends, they [the manufacturers] and their agents in unmeasured terms denounced the public school as behind the age, as inefficient, as lacking in public spirit. . . . The arrogance of the manufacturers was two-fold—first in condemning the schools for not doing what thinking men had never before considered it the duty of the schools to do and what the traditions of thousands of years laid upon the manufacturers to do; and second, in demanding that the state should then proceed to pay the bills for training their workmen.[18]

The great social and educational reformer Jane Addams, writing in a spirit of true Christian charity, also had a few words to say on this topic in 1897:

> The businessman has, of course, not said to himself "I will have the public school train office boys and clerks for me so that I may have them cheap," but he has thought, and sometimes said, "Teach the children to write legibly, to figure accurately, to acquire habits of punctuality and order, to be prompt, to obey, and not question why; and you will fit them to make their way in the world as I have made mine."[19]

This new decontextualized approach of formal vocational schooling conducted inside the walls of a schoolhouse led to the creation of a large number of trade schools, technical institutes, and agricultural colleges, including the great land-grant universities established in every state of the union. While in many ways this constituted a dramatic expansion of this country's technological knowledge, it also led to such strange anomalies as the spending of large quantities of public tax money to build in schools duplicates of the real world's auto repair shops, sheet metal shops, woodworking shops, bakeries, upholstery shops, electrical shops, plumbing shops, business offices, kitchens, and sewing rooms and attempting to train students in that artificial environment to perform real-world tasks.

To make matters worse, those in-school "vocational" facilities have over the years and in all too many cases been poorly supported financially and thus have almost always lagged technologically far behind their real-world models. They have therefore produced large numbers of poorly educated graduates adept at using yesterday's tools. This fact seems not to have served to make everyone, and especially the leaders of business and industry, raise their taxes to bring the schools up to date but has instead primarily been a cause for complaint about the low quality of public education on the part of the very members of business and industry who saddled the schools with this responsibility in the first place.

The Birth of the Two Incompatible Systems

When we began to establish this broader system of American public schooling in the late 19th century, it appeared to many of the educational thinkers who emerged in that period at both higher and lower educational levels that the state of the established system—especially as it was practiced in our large urban school systems—was hopelessly ramshackle, disorderly, inefficient, of very low quality, decidedly unprofessional, profoundly unrationalized, and therefore thoroughly "unscientific." One of their principal and often fully justified complaints was that tax-supported public schooling was rife with political meddling and graft, on the basis in part of the idea that anyone who had a modicum of schooling was obviously qualified to be a teacher—especially the sons, daughters, nieces, nephews, husbands, wives, and girl-, and boyfriends of local politicians.

Not only were lines of authority unclear, but there was a distressing lack of uniformity in school system management. The higher education people were disturbed because there was no carefully worked-out, standardized method for judging whether students were actually academically well-trained and thus suitable college material.

The public—and especially the business and industrial community—was concerned because there was no generally agreed-upon way to determine just how much the public schools were costing the taxpayers and whether the public was getting its money's worth.[20]

The response of the higher education community to the academic, high school part of this challenge in 1893 was to turn the matter over to Charles W. Eliot, the president of Harvard University, and the Committee of Ten of the National Education Association. Although Eliot's committee did recommend a broadening of the high school curriculum to include a greater emphasis on the sciences and "vocational" education and the addition of some subjects as "electives," the primary result was to reaffirm and codify the central importance of the established separate and distinct disciplinary "core" academic subjects, especially as the study of these subjects was declared to be the proper way to prepare a small number of elitely selected students to enter the world of higher education and the socially powerful, high-paying professions.[21]

It was this authoritarian pressure from higher academe that reified those academic subject compartments and led eventually to the mechanical quantification system of "Carnegie units" and "grade point averages," to the College Board examinations in those separated subjects and to the Scholastic Aptitude Test (the SAT, now more properly renamed the Scholastic Assessment Test). It is certainly true that these tests were in part aimed at making sure that "academically talented" students of any social class were discovered and admitted to college, if necessary with scholarship help. But the primary result of the tests was—in the grand Jeffersonian tradition—to identify those students, almost entirely, male, White, and well-to-do, who were clearly qualified (all too often purely by family wealth, ancestral institutional attendance, or both) to meet the relatively standardized academic college admissions requirements. These requirements were based largely upon the successful passing of tests in the established scholarly subject matter disciplines as they were taught in the country's colleges and universities and therefore in the country's high schools.

The Creation and Growing Dominance of the Industrial Model in American Schooling

But a quite radical change was occurring at this time in a wide spectrum of American social and economic institutions, very much including both secondary and elementary public schooling. This was the application of a new approach to institutional management, the technocratic dream of the perfect, rational, well-ordered, impersonal, eminently predictable machine of social and economic control, the social and educational equivalent of the Newtonian clockwork universe. This was the doctrine of "scientific management" and its associated psychological doctrine of mechanistic behaviorism.[22]

The high priest of this new breed of industrial "scientific managers" was Frederick W. Taylor, who was by profession a university-trained mechanical engineer. His new industrial system was "rationally"—and therefore "scientifically"—designed to wring the greatest possible productivity from human labor, and this worthy end could be achieved, he believed, only by applying rational, systematic and impersonal "scientific" principles to the processes of industrial production.

Taylor saw a new role for industrial managers—the task of analyzing, planning, and controlling every aspect, every detail, of the manufacturing process with the aim of producing the greatest degree of output from human beings in the most efficient and cost-effective manner possible and thus yielding the greatest possible profit to the owners of the industry. Every factory in the new industrial system was to be organized as a strict hierarchy with the managers on top making all the decisions and each worker down below carefully trained to carry out those decisions by doing one precise, endlessly repetitive task and only that precise task.

This philosophy gave birth to the "efficiency expert" and the "time/motion study" in which the manager, stopwatch in hand, laid down precisely what every worker in the factory was supposed to do at every moment of the day and precisely how long it was to take that worker to do it. Once this had been figured out, all jobs were then standardized throughout the factory. Every worker had such a single standardized task to perform on the raw material used by the plant. It was the worker's job to perform his or her assigned task precisely in the way it was designed to be done by the managers. It was the manager's job to do the "thinking and planning" and the worker's job to do precisely what he or she was told to do.

This industrial approach to production, however, was not limited to the manufacturing industries. It extended also into such other fields as agriculture. The wine historian Matt Kramer describes this application of what he calls the "machine in the mind" approach to agriculture and wine. Beginning in the 1930s, he says:

> agricultural colleges everywhere were locked in a battle with farmers. Professors at agricultural colleges were dedicated to applying to agriculture the same principles of "systemization" that was the idée fixe of America from the 1870's to the 1920's. The idea of systemization was applied to virtually all business and social endeavors. Farming was no exception. These systematic agriculturalists . . . assumed that farming was composed of numerous discrete operations and that success was the consequence of rationally conceived and pursued methods.[23]

The agricultural colleges, says Kramer, were "subsidized by those businesses with an interest in the benefits to be reaped by large scale farming performed with mechanical reliability and predictability." In the field of winemaking, this led for many decades to huge wineries and the massive production of low-quality bulk wines (such as Gallo's Hearty Burgundy). For the first time, vineyards were established and operated not by the traditional, historic wedding of hands and minds that had produced the great wines of Europe (and all the great cuisines of the world) "but by scientific methodology. It was rational. It was systematic.."

It was not, says Kramer, until the 1970s with the gradual growth of interest in California in the production of high-quality wines to rival those of France and Italy that the winemakers began to realize that this "machine in the mind" approach was simply not applicable to a biological system such as the making of fine wines. Such wines could only be made, they discovered, as they were in Europe, in smaller vineyards where great attention was paid to the unsystematic, unpredictable, "ambiguous" details that suited each individual grape variety—such as the exact type of soil, just the right amount of irrigation, the distance between vines, how the vines are terraced, and when and how the grapes should be picked as well as the myriad possibilities involved in the actual fermenting, aging, and bottling of the wine at the winery. Only if the machine-in-the-mind mentality was set aside and replaced by this down-to-earth, strictly biological and essentially artistic approach could the present great Californian wines be produced.[24]

Those ruling ideas of systematic, "scientific" efficiency, however, in the early days of the past century were not limited to agriculture or our industrial factories. Those methods were quickly adopted by the educational establishment as the right and proper way, the professional and scientific way, to depoliticize and more efficiently run a public school system.

The application of these principles to our system of public schooling enabled Elwood P. Cubberley, one of the country's leading educators at the time and a strong proponent of such an application, to say as early as 1916:

> Our schools are, in a sense, factories, in which the raw products [children] are to be shaped and fashioned into products to meet the various demands of life. The specifications for manufacturing come from the demands of twentieth century civilization, and it is the business of the school to build its pupils to the specifications laid down. This demands good tools, specialized machinery, continuous measurement of production to see if it is according to specifications, the elimination of waste in manufacture and a large variety of output.[25]

Following this technocratic/scientific industrial model, the educational theorists early in the 20th century declared that our school systems should also be organized as strict, unyielding, authoritarian, machine-in-the-mind hierarchies, with all basic decisions about how the enterprise should be conducted made by the local school board (acting as an industrial board of directors) and by the top managers of the system.

These decisions were then to be passed down through a rigidly policed bureaucracy to each level below. Each level of the system—middle-manager bureaucrats, white-collar office workers and the teachers out in the schools who were the equivalent of the workers on the assembly lines—had specific tasks assigned to them. Out in the schools, the job of the teachers was to follow orders from above and perform their allotted tasks and no others. All such teacher/workers were assumed to be replaceable cogs in the total-production machine. Students—the raw material fed into the school factories—were organized into rigid grade structures, and what they should be taught and how they were supposed to learn it were also spelled out in great detail and then tested on the universal standardized academic achievement tests.

This right and proper way to run a school system became the predominant way throughout the country in the years that followed. And here the marriage of the professional leaders of the school hierarchies and Charles Eliot's academic scholars of the world of higher education came into full bloom. For it has been those scholarly experts in the traditional academic disciplines, with their disciplinary prescriptions and their Carnegie units, SAT tests, grade point averages, and college entrance requirements, who have largely determined what will be taught in the schools.

It has been the academic higher education experts in each discipline, assisted by "subject matter curricular specialists" down in the school systems, who have been hired by the corporate leaders of the textbook-publishing industry to write the textbooks in each core subject. These textbooks then in turn essentially determine what the curriculum of the lower schools will contain at each grade level, along with "teacher guides" describing how students should be instructed in each subject at each grade level.

This industrial educational process begins with assignment of all children and young people to their age-appropriate educational level—an elementary school, junior high or middle school, or high school, preferably in or near each student's "neighborhood"—followed immediately by their being sorted into classes according to their age, with all 5-year-olds assigned to kindergarten classes, all 6-year-olds to "first grade" classes, all 7-year-olds to "second grade" classes and so on up through high school.

Although the scientific-management educators did not invent this process of age grading (the first age-graded school was Boston's Quincy School, built in 1848 and still extant, although no longer used as a school), they refined its application by spelling out in great detail what every child should learn in each grade and by spelling out as well the precise, step-by-step sequence of lessons, exercises, and drills by which each skill and each segment of subject matter was to be presented to students by the teacher at each grade level. Thus the "raw products," the children, were to be fed into the process at age 5 and systematically "shaped and fashioned" year by year in accordance with the system's mission "to build its pupils to the specifications laid down."

Part of this shaping and fashioning process was often—and is still often—the practice of "ability grouping" or "tracking" within each grade level. When they enter school or shortly thereafter, students are given IQ or academic achievement tests or both and are sorted into separate classes or "tracks" depending on the test results—and often in no small measure depending on whether their teachers think of them as being very smart, average smart, or not so smart (shades of my K–8 school and Mr. Black's class).

Once this industrial model has been set in place, it is then the job of the central administrators at the top of the hierarchy to pass all the organizational and curricular decisions on down the line to the principals and teachers in the individual schools, which historically have been the so-called neighborhood school down the street. It has in turn been the job of the principals and teachers to run their schools according to the directives issued from central headquarters, with each school being roughly like every other school. Each school thus becomes an individual "factory" in the system and each classroom a "work station" on the factory's educational assembly line. The teacher/worker assigned to each classroom work station is given a set of instructions on how to operate the classroom so that the "specifications laid down" will be met.

In their turn, the teachers and principals have had the job of informing the parents of their students about what is to be taught and how it is to be taught, what "track" their children will be assigned to and therefore how "smart" each of those children is considered to be and thus what expectations both the school and the parents should have for each of those children both in school and in life, what the promotional standards for students will be, and so on. Although this is the ideal the system designers had in mind, it has not always worked out quite that way in real schools where caring teachers often subvert the rigors of the system and do pay attention to student idiosyncrasies. Parents for the most part have had no opportunity to be directly involved in any of these decisions. If parents wanted to have such a say over their children's education, they would had have to somehow manage to pay tuition at private or parochial schools, obtaining the kind of control always enjoyed by wealthy parents.

The central administrators must also adopt and put into practice a series of quality-control devices, most often in the form of standardized, norm-referenced and usually multiple-choice achievement tests for each grade level, to see whether all the skills and subject matter that children and young people are supposed to learn are actually and successfully being taught. This has been

the educational equivalent of industry's (and Cubberley's) "continuous measurement of production to see if it is according to specifications."

The Educational and Social Results
of This Industrial Model

What this typical American public school system inevitably became was
and still is a system that—in no small measure as a result of the practice of
"tracking"—reflects and tends to reify the social class structure of American
society. While it is true that the system has also rescued many lower-class children and given them a chance to succeed in life well beyond their social-class
expectations, over the years many educational researchers, including sociolo-
gist and educational researcher Richard Rothstein of the Economic Policy
Institute, have consistently pointed out that it is in no small measure this educational system that makes it very difficult for poor and minority students to
succeed in school when success is determined almost solely by standardized
test score results. It is a well-known fact that both IQ scores and academic
test scores are closely correlated with a student's social class. Low-income and
minority children consistently score several "grade levels" below middle- and
upper-class children and are thus routinely placed in a school's lower "tracks."
Indeed, the best predictor of any student's eventual test score (and therefore
school) achievement in these conventional schools is the social and educational
level of that student's parents.[26]

Rothstein also produces strong evidence showing that the low test scores
of poor and minority children are not the result of any innate, unalterable cognitive skill deficits (a fact we believed we also discovered for ourselves at the
Boardman), but of the social and environmental factors involved in being poor.
The basic handicap here is simply that the parents of poor children do not have
an adequate income to support a family, this being the result of the enormous,
unjust disparities in the distribution of this country's wealth. For poor families
this income disparity results all too often in inadequate health and preschool
services; poor nutrition; inadequate housing, including the possibility of lead
paint poisoning; no timely detection of vision and hearing problems; lack of
learning materials in the home; and so on, all of which factors combine to ensure poor performance not only in school but also in later life.[27]

The classic remedy for this test score disparity—or what has come to be
called that "achievement gap"—has been "compensatory education," that is,
giving the low-income, low-track children additional and more intensive "instruction" in reading and math to improve their scores while systematically
reducing the time spent on all the other subject areas that the non-"disadvantaged" students were still receiving.

The Simultaneous Advent of the Progressive Model

At the same time as this industrial model was being put in place during the late 19th and early 20th centuries, both this country and England saw the birth of the new "progressive" movement, primarily in private schools but also in some sectors of public education.

In this country, as the general progressive move toward greater democratization of the economic and political processes gained strength, so too did the movement led by Francis W. Parker, John Dewey, Maria Montessori, William James, Jane Addams, and many others to create a new, more humane, child-centered model of educating the young that had begun to be advocated in England by the likes of Robert Owen and Alfred Wallace, and in Europe by Johann Pestalozzi and Fredrich Froebel, a movement that was aimed at radically and democratically transforming both private and public schooling.

When Parker was named superintendent of schools in Quincy, Massachusetts, in 1873, according to Cremin:

> things soon began to happen. The set curriculum was abandoned, and with it the speller, the reader, the grammar, and the copy book. Children started on simple words and sentences, rather than the alphabet learned by rote. In place of time-honored texts, magazines, newspapers, and materials devised by the teachers themselves were introduced into the classroom. Arithmetic was approached inductively, through objects rather than rules, while geography began with a series of trips over the local countryside. Drawing was added to encourage manual dexterity and individual expression. The emphasis was on observing, describing, and understanding, and only when these abilities had begun to manifest themselves—among the faculty as well as the students—were more conventional studies introduced.

Parker, who had studied Pestalozzi and Froebel in Europe, took all these ideas with him when he moved from Quincy to the Cook County Normal School in Chicago. Here, again according to Cremin, Parker's techniques of informality prevailed.

> For reading and writing, the children created their own stories, and these, in the form of "Reading Leaflets" printed at the school, quickly replaced primers and textbooks. Spelling, reading, penmanship, and grammar were all thus combined as elements of communication, to be studied within the context of actual conversation and writing. Drill was recognized as a necessity, but always in the context of more immediate student interests.

Although Parker knew nothing of the great Paleolithic cave artists (Lascaux in France was not discovered until 1940), he made art a central part of the school experience, arguing that modeling, painting, and drawing were "three great steps in the evolution of man."

Science, according to Cremin, began with nature study, with field trips conducted in neighboring fields and lakes, and was correlated with language and art through observations, drawings, and written descriptions. Students carried the results of these exercises back into the classroom laboratories and into more formal studies in biology and physics. Math was often introduced as part of this lab work. Geography, economics, history, music, drama, hygiene, and physical education were all seen as vehicles for students expressing themselves and all began with what had meaning for the children themselves.[28]

When John Dewey joined the faculty at the University of Chicago in 1894, it was his visit to Parker's school that led him to establish his famous Laboratory School at the university and to begin his lifelong espousal of the theory and practice of truly democratic, progressive education.

After World War I, these "pedagogical pioneers," as Cremin calls them,[29] created what he labels that "progressive era in education," the period between 1917 and 1957 when the ideas espoused by the pioneers began to have an ameliorating effect on the authoritarian rigors of the traditional, industrial-management schools. Spearheaded by Dewey when he moved to Columbia University's Teachers College in New York City, progressive ideas began to infiltrate and somewhat humanize the practices of Taylor's industrial model school system.

In England, a similar movement was under way well before 1900, pioneered by Owen at his New Lanark model industrial community in the early 1800s. Here is Wallace's account of Owen's schools:

> Owen founded his society on the educational system he invented for its children. He built handsome and roomy schools, complete with playrooms and lecture rooms for infants from two to six, and for older children from six to ten. He sought out and hired the best teachers for the latter. He told those teachers that they were on no account ever to beat any one of the children, or threaten them in any manner in word or action, or to use abusive terms, but were always to speak to them with a pleasant countenance and in a kind manner and tone of voice. They should tell the infants and children that they must on all occasions do all they could to make their playfellows happy; and that the older children, from five to six years of age, should take especial care of the younger ones, and should assist and teach them to make each other happy.
>
> The children were to be taught the uses and nature or qualities of common things around them by familiar conversation when the children's curiosity was excited so as to induce them to ask questions respecting them. The schoolrooms were furnished with paintings of natural objects, and the children were also taught dancing, singing and military evolutions, which they greatly enjoyed. The children were never kept at any one occupation or amusement till they were tired

and were taken as often as possible into the open air and into the surrounding country, where they were taught about every natural object. These were the essential features of the educational system developed on the continent by Rousseau, Hebart, Pestalozzi and Froebel, but Owen arrived at them through his own observations of children, beginning with his own experiences as a child and as an assistant teacher in his own early schooling.[30]

These early English explorations were followed in the 20th century by the psychological work of Piaget, Vygotsky, and Nathan and Susan Isaacs and gradually spread into many English schools. The efforts led to the 1967 two-volume Plowden Report, *Children and Their Primary Schools,* a government publication that spelled out the new approach in considerable detail. These new methods began to be widely practiced by the many teachers out in the schools who were gradually coming to believe, as one education official put it, that school should be "a place where children can grow." Eventually, these "child centered" practices began to spread into many—but certainly not all—primary and junior schools when, after World War II, in some county systems such as that of Leicestershire, "informal" education began to become the norm.[31]

The Fundamental Noneffects of American Progressivism

There is little doubt that Darwin and Wallace would have been pleased to see the changes wrought by the progressives in both England and the United States during the century just passed, and it is certainly true that the proponents of progressive schooling have had an ameliorating effect on the rigidities of the "scientifically managed" schools. But the unfortunate fact was—and still is—that truly progressive schooling practices in this country have been found primarily not in our public systems but in the private schools. The leading examples here have often been such private schools attached to teacher-training institutions, including Dewey's Chicago Lab School, the Lincoln School attached to Teachers College, and schools connected to the Bank Street College of Education. But there was also a flourishing movement of progressive independent private schools such as Shady Hill in Cambridge, Massachusetts, the Little Red Schoolhouse and Elizabeth Irwin in New York City, and many Montessori schools that have almost always had to be private.

A few public school systems briefly made such schooling the norm during Cremin's "progresssive era"—systems such as those of Gary, Indiana; Winnetka, Illinois; and Pasadena, California. But the central fact has been that only a minority of American public elementary and secondary schools, either then or now, could be legitimately classified as truly progressive, as was proved to me by the unprogressive schools I attended, the equally unprogressive ones I visited during my Ford Foundation days, and also the many schools I have worked with in subsequent years consulting with school districts all across the country as I attempted with distinctly limited success to encourage the creation of such schools.

One Certification of the Success: The 8-Year Study

There is some evidence, however, that during this period the progressive educators in this country did succeed in what they were trying to do—if "success" here is measured not by whether all this country's schools became progressive (which they certainly did not) but by the limited goal of whether the graduates of such schools went on to succeed in higher education.

The most important such evidence is contained in what came to be called the 8-Year Study, conducted in the 1930s and early 1940s by the Commission on the Relation of School and College of the Progressive Education Association (PEA).

The problem facing the advocates of progressive education and thus the PEA in 1930 was the question of college admissions requirements. The PEA's executive board appointed a committee "to explore the possibilities of better coordination of school and college work and to seek an agreement which would provide freedom for secondary schools to attempt fundamental reconstruction."

The committee decided that they wished "to work toward a type of secondary education which will be flexible, responsive to changing needs, and clearly based on an understanding of the qualities needed in adult life. We are trying to develop students who regard education as an enduring quest for meanings rather than credit accumulation; who desire to investigate, to follow the leadings of a subject, to explore new fields of thought; knowing how to budget time, to read well, to use sources of knowledge effectively and who are experienced in fulfilling obligations which come with membership in the school or college community." A splendid description, in short, of what progressive schooling is all about.

But would such schools be able to get their students admitted to the country's colleges and universities? To answer that question, the commission set up an elaborate experiment. Thirty high schools across the country, public and private, representing a cross section of the high school population, were selected to develop themselves into the "fundamentally reconstructed" progressive schools they had always wished and hoped to become. Some 300 colleges were then organized to waive their normal admissions requirements for graduates of these schools. The success or failure of the experiment would then be determined by how well the progressively educated students did in college.

The assessment team's technique was to set up 1,475 pairs of college students, each consisting of a graduate of one of the study schools and a graduate of some other nonprogressive secondary school matched as closely as possible with respect to sex, age, race, scholastic aptitude scores, home and community background, and vocational and avocational interest.

At the end of the study 8 years later, the assessment team reported the following results for the students admitted from the 30 progressive schools when compared with the graduates of nonprogressive schools: They earned a slightly higher total grade average; they displayed a greater degree of intellectual curiosity and drive; they seemed to have developed clearer ideas concerning the meaning of education; they more often demonstrated a high degree of resourcefulness in meeting new situations; they had about the same problems of adjustment to college life as the comparison group but approached the solution to the problem with greater effectiveness; they participated more and more frequently in organized student groups; they earned a higher percentage of nonacademic honors; they had a somewhat better orientation toward a choice of vocation; and they demonstrated a more active concern with national and world affairs. All the results, in short, that the progressives could possibly hope for.[32]

One might have thought that such results would immediately have a transformative effect both on the nation's high schools and on college admissions requirements. The results were totally ignored, in part, no doubt, because they appeared in 1942, during World War II, a time when the nation's attention and efforts were hardly directed at the improvement of its public schools.

An even more important reason for the disregard of the study and its results, however, is that the radically progressive educational changes were limited to the experiment's high schools. The higher education institutions engaged in the study were asked only to lift temporarily their traditional admissions requirements, not to change themselves into progressive colleges and universities that would therefore be institutions that would be hospitable to and continue to encourage such improved educational results. This was the case even though the students from the progressive schools clearly demonstrated that the progressive educational methods produced better results by the colleges' own standards. If those students had been able to attend equally progressive colleges, their results might have been even more impressive.

But perhaps most important of all, those institutions of higher education did not exert pressure on the nation's other high schools or on public education in general to become more "progressive," even though they had evidence that the graduates of the progressive schools "did better" in college than did the graduates of traditional schools.

The Destruction of Progressivism

Meanwhile, in the 1970s and 1980s both in this country and in Britain, the antiprogressive back-to-basics movement that had begun in the Sputnik era picked up steam. This gradual abandonment in England of the Plowden Report's progressive practices has been described by Derek Gillard, a long-time teacher and educational critic:

> In 1976, it became clear that politicians wanted to take greater control of the school curriculum. . . . Political forces began to shape curriculum thinking and development. Notions of core, common and national curriculum all seemed to have at their root the idea that children were to be fitted to the service of the state or at least to fulfill their allotted roles in society. . . . Significantly, Plowden's view that "At the heart of the educational process lies the child" was abandoned in favour of "The school curriculum is at the heart of education."

When the Conservative Party took power in 1979, Gillard says, Prime Minister Margaret Thatcher "sought to turn the public education service into a market place." The culmination of this movement "was the 1988 Education 'Reform' Act, which, with its imposition of a subject-based National Curriculum and its associated regime of testing and published league tables [test results by school], forced schools to train pupils to get good test results so as to compete for pupils."

What has ensued is regrettable, says Gillard:

> New Labour has continued to embrace this approach to education with even more tests, targets and divisive elitism. . . . Plowden is a voice from the past but one which urgently needs a hearing again today. When politicians realise that that what is measurable is not all that is valuable, when teachers begin to notice that children learn nothing by being tested, when parents are sick of their young children suffering from exam-induced stress, when the public begins to realize that the results of national tests can always be manipulated to achieve politicians' targets, and when decent people decide to stand up against the shame-and-name culture of failure, then someone, somewhere, is going to remember that "at the heart of the educational process lies the child."[33]

There is a possibility, however, that Plowden may be making a comeback: In 2006 the Association of Teachers and Lecturers, the largest English teachers union, called for the abandonment of the national curriculum and an end to all national testing before the age of 16. As the general secretary of the union, Dr. Mary Bousted, has put it, "We need to give teachers the freedom to inspire youngsters so they want to learn, not just pass tests. We also need pupils to have the space to develop as rounded people, and that includes physically, emotionally, creatively, socially and ethically."[34]

In this country the antiprogressive movement was powerfully advanced by the 1983 publication of the U.S. Department of Education's widely heralded *A Nation at Risk* report.[35] This report was created by the National Commission on Excellence in Education, set up by Secretary of Education Terrell Bell, in the administration of President Ronald Reagan, to investigate "the widespread public perception that something is seriously amiss in our educational system." The 18-member commission was, with the exception of one principal and one teacher, made up entirely of nonschool people—university academics, corporate executives, school board members, and politicians.

It was this report that famously claimed that "the educational foundations of our society are presently being eroded by a rising tide of mediocrity that threatens our very future as a nation and a people." Other countries, the report maintained, were surpassing us in "educational attainment" and thus were also threatening to surpass us economically and culturally. "If an unfriendly foreign power had attempted to impose on America the mediocre educational performance that exists today," said the report, "we might well have viewed it as an act of war."

To support these charges, the commission assembled a mass of scholarly educational research data, almost all of it based upon the results of national and international standardized test score results claiming to show that while these scores had declined in this country they were rising in other industrialized nations. This mass of data, the report claimed, documented the comparatively widespread educational mediocrity in our educational system and the subsequent dangers to our competitive position in the world economy.

To redress this situation, the report went on to make five general recommendations:

1. that state and local high school graduation requirements be strengthened by requiring all students seeking a diploma to take 4 years of English, 4 years of math, 3 years of science, 3 years of social studies and ½ year of computer science, plus 2 years of a foreign language for the college bound;
2. that schools, colleges, and universities adopt more rigorous and measurable standards and higher expectations for academic performance and student conduct, and that 4-year colleges and universities raise their requirements for admission;
3. that significantly more time be devoted to learning the new diploma requirements with a more effective use of the school day, a longer school day, or a longer school year;

4. that the standards for teacher education be made more rigorous, that teacher salaries be raised, that teachers have an 11-month contract and a career ladder, that nonschool personnel be recruited to help teach science and math, and that master teachers help design teacher education programs and mentor beginning teachers;

5. that citizens across the nation hold educators and elected officials responsible for providing the leadership and fiscal support necessary to achieve all these reforms.

Needless to say, the report provoked storms of both praise and outrage. The praise came primarily from the business and corporate communities, from some segments of higher education, and from the critics, of all stripes, who had been most vociferous in condemning the excesses of progressive schooling. The outrage came largely from members of the public education establishment, particularly from the teacher and administrator unions; from many members of the educational research community; and from progressive educators throughout the land.

The first national results of the *Nation at Risk* report were the holding of three "national educational summit" meetings, one in the administration of President George H. W. Bush and two during the time of President Bill Clinton. These summits were convened under the aegis of the National Governors Association in cooperation with federal education officials and conservative school people and most especially with the powerful support of corporate CEOs such as those from IBM and RJR Nabisco.

These summits called for a massive setting of new, "world class" academic standards in all the conventional subject matter disciplines, to be accompanied by a system of "high stakes" standardized testing to make sure that students were not socially promoted from one grade level to the next or graduated from high school until they had thoroughly absorbed all the orthodox subject matter and passed all the orthodox tests.

Those summit messages were translated by the Bush I and Clinton administrations into the national educational agenda, called Goals 2000, based on those "high" academic standards and "high stakes" standardized testing, the agenda that began to be carried out by every state in the union except Iowa. These states thus began the process of setting such strictly academic standards for all public school students and imposing such strictly academic tests on all students, all teachers, all schools, and all parents in public schools throughout the country.

However, the ultimate blow came in 2001 when one of the first congressional initiatives of the administration of President George W. Bush, the so-called No Child Left Behind Act (NCLB, which in its original proposed form did contain a voucher proposal), was passed by both Republican and

Democratic members of Congress (but without the voucher scheme). This
act requires that any state willing to accept the federal money must set those
high, "world class" academic standards in reading and mathematics (and eventually in all the orthodox subject matter categories) beginning in the preschool
years and running through to high school graduation. These standards must
then be accompanied by high-stakes standardized tests administered each year
to assess whether the standards are being met.

These state standards and the accompanying tests are then imposed on all
school districts and all schools within the state if the local districts in their turn
agree to accept the federal funding. Then, as the test results are examined,
each school in the district is rated as a success, as a school that "needs improvement," or as a failure on the basis of how many of its students score as
"proficient" on the tests. Schools that are not rated as successful are then expected to show improvement in their test scores every year ("average yearly
progress") until all students achieve some arbitrary level of "proficiency." If a
school does not accomplish this, it can be either closed or taken over by the
state and "reconstituted" with a new staff. Meanwhile, students in a "failing"
school can demand to be transferred to a more "successful" one, whether there
are available seats in the school or not.

Coercion and "Meanness" as a National Education Policy

The Bush No Child Left Behind agenda is technically not a federal mandate, but rather a federal bribe. No state or district is required to buy into
the program if it is willing to forego the federal money. But it is being treated
as a mandate by every state and most (but not all) local districts who desperately need and therefore are eager to get the federal money. This is the case
even though it has become starkly apparent that the financial requirements
of the act—and especially the costs of the enormous increase in standardized testing—far exceed any funding the act brings in. For instance, the
Congress's Government Accountability Office has estimated that states will
have to spend up to $6.5 billion over the coming 6 years just on tests and
testing.[36] Meanwhile, the amount of money actually appropriated by the Bush
administration and the Republican Congress has been billions short of what
the congressional sponsors of the bill originally authorized and thus far short
of what would be required to cover all the program's additional costs.

But critics of NCLB have an even greater range of serious doubts about
its wisdom. The National Center for Fair and Open Testing (FairTest), perhaps the nation's leading authority on the matter, has launched a national
campaign critical of NCLB. The center's specific criticisms begin with two
"false" assumptions underlying the act:

- that boosting standardized test scores should be the primary goal of the schools (arguing that this leads to one size-fits-all teaching aimed solely at test preparation and thus against efforts to give all children a high-quality education);
- that schools can be improved through educators being threatened with harsh sanctions (arguing that schools alone can never overcome the social problems of family poverty and inadequate school funding).[37]

This reliance on coercion and "meanness" as the basis for a national education policy is defended by many of the agenda's conservative proponents, such as the American Enterprise Institute's Frederick Hess, who sets forth a dichotomy between what he calls "nice" educational accountability, which emphasizes providing schools with more adequate resources, and "mean" accountability, which relies almost solely on standardized testing and punishments for schools that fail to measure up on their test score results (which is what he strongly supports). "In such a system," he says, "school performance no longer rests on fond wishes and good intentions. Instead, such levers as diplomas and job security are used to compel students and teachers to cooperate. Mean accountability seeks to harness the self-interest of students and educators to refocus schools and redefine the expectations of teachers and learners."[38]

According to FairTest:

What makes NCLB so dangerous is the way it links standardized testing with heavy sanctions through the rigid "adequate yearly progress" formula. Thus the weakness of standardized exams—their cultural biases and their failure to measure higher order thinking—are reinforced by strict penalties. The consequence of narrow exams and strong sanctions is intensive teaching to the test. This response undermines decent education as well as efforts to ensure improvements in genuine educational quality.[39] (FairTest's recommendations for a more humane accountability scheme are described in Chapter 5.)

One thing that FairTest is pointing out here is NCLB's Lake Wobegon insistence that all students must eventually score at least at an "average" level of "proficiency" and preferably well above it. It as if major league baseball suddenly decreed that within the next 5 years every major league player must have a .350 batting average, including National League pitchers who are not prized for their hitting skills as well as American League pitchers who are clearly "handicapped" by not being allowed to bat at all. If any team during that 5-year period could not demonstrate that every batter each year is making adequate yearly progress toward that impossible proficiency goal of .350, that team could be shut down and replaced by a new one. Meanwhile, players on the poor teams could transfer to the better-performing teams whether there was a position for them to play or not.

One of this country's leading researchers, Gerald W. Bracey, a fellow for the High/Scope Educational Research Foundation, who writes the monthly research column for the respected educational journal *Phi Delta Kappan*, has spent the past 20 years strenuously criticizing both the quality and the conclusions of the research used in the *Nation at Risk* report as well as the research that this general antiprogressive movement has relied upon. Not only was most of that research either wrong or willfully misinterpreted, according to Bracey, but the critics routinely ignore a large body of research indicating that if one is willing to use only test scores as a criterion (which no good progressive educator would ever do), American schools have actually come out at or near the top on international comparisons.

Bracey—along with many other critics of the movement—has also taken the movement to task for relying almost solely on standardized test scores as the lone criterion for judging the quality of any country's educational system.[40] None of these critics, however, is saying that just because our test scores do measure up to international scores this means that the existing American system of public schooling is the best one we could or should have.

Indeed, this is a system that could not be worse for the poor and minority children whom the antiprogressive movement and especially NCLB claim to be helping by attempting to close the "achievement gap."

To return for a moment to the Boardman example, we had considerable anecdotal evidence that most of those "poor and minority" children who started early and continued at the Boardman began to do quite well in all the ways we were hoping they would on a broad range of cognitive skills, such as the ability to use their minds well and become enthralled by such use, to think clearly, to reason well, to discover and solve problems, and to develop their epistemological understanding.

But we also thought we saw many instances when they were doing well on a host of other skills, talents, and attributes—whether they were displaying previously unnoticed talents in music, the arts, and science; whether they really were developing initiative and responsibility for their own learning; whether they were becoming people who cared about one another; whether they were beginning to see themselves as competent, capable human beings able to think for themselves; and whether they were beginning to see the act of inquiring and learning as a satisfying and rewarding experience in and of itself, something they could learn to love, and not simply dreary "school" drudgery. Admittedly, we could well have been hopelessly biased here, but as with the manifest successes the students were having in the classes of Ms. Jackson and Ms. Fitzgerald, we were, I think, genuinely convinced that all these good things were really happening for most of our students.

And the students also appeared to be doing quite well on our value-added standardized-testing routine. Unfortunately, the subsystem experiment did not continue long enough to give us any longitudinal data on the children who started at the Boardman and might eventually have made it all the way through the high school and, we devoutly hoped and expected, would then go on to college. But we certainly did come to at least the tentative conclusion that simply giving low-income and minority children more instruction and more intensive instruction in basic skills is not the way to give them the education they need and deserve.

But not just the education that low-income and minority students need and deserve. What eventually became utterly clear to us in the subsystem was that the conventional instructional, industrial model of education was not the way to educate any student—poor, rich, or in between. And we also saw that it was especially not the kind of education that should be practiced in any society that was calling itself a democracy and claimed to be attempting to make itself more democratic by increasingly empowering all its citizenry through its system of public education. It was, rather, a system of schooling based on Jane Addams's acquisition of "habits of punctuality and order, to be prompt, to obey, and not to question why," a system, as Cubberley approvingly described it, that was specifically designed to produce a compliant, docile citizenry that would be content with and therefore content to serve the existing social, political, and economic order.

The Dangers of the Move Toward Privatization

It also important to note here that although the 1983 *Nation at Risk* report was praised at a press conference by Reagan and his administration, it did not follow the stated educational agenda of that administration. In previous statements, Reagan had called for an educational reform program that was based essentially on providing parents with the financial means to avoid the public schools entirely through tax-supported educational vouchers and tuition tax credits, enabling them to send their children to private (including religious) schools. He also advocated returning prayer to the remaining public schools and abolishing the federal Department of Education.

The Reagan agenda was the official beginning at the federal level of what many supporters of public schooling see as a powerful campaign on the part of the conservative and largely (although by no means exclusively) Republican Right to turn public education over not only to the existing and most typically nonprofit private schools—including religious schools—but also to the private corporate sector by allowing public vouchers and tax credits to be used to pay tuition at a growing network of corporately run, for-profit private schools. This for-profit corporate approach to public schooling has also been applied to state or locally run charter schools, many of which have been subcontracted to the private, for-profit sector. This practice has even been extended to the running of local district schools, thus adding fuel to the argument that the ultimate aim of this movement is to replace the public school system with a basically private one.

And NCLB is clearly the newest and most frightening danger in this privatization campaign. In addition to allowing federal funds to be used to hire for-profit private tutoring companies to tutor low-achieving students, the law specifically enables states and districts with "failing" schools not only to take over and "reconstitute" them with new staff but, if they so desire, also to contract them out to be run by private, for-profit "educational maintenance organizations" (the new EMOs, to match the HMOs [health maintenance organizations] of the health care system) such as the Edison Schools Corporation.

For instance, the U.S. Department of Education in its December 2004 *Education Innovator* newsletter, specifically promoted for-profit Edison, saying that "sometimes an expert has to be brought in to help in the education community" and that "help from an outside 'educational management organization' [an EMO] can be a way to solve problems" that cannot be solved by the local education authorities. The newsletter goes on to say that Edison now serves 250,000 students (26,000 in charter schools) and that it has significantly raised test scores in many low-income schools, claims that Gerald Bracey and many others have consistently refuted.[41]

Nowhere does the newsletter, an official publication of a federal department supported by public tax money, mention that Edison and other corporate "EMOs" are in the education business to make money. Nor does the department anywhere raise the question of whether it is morally legitimate for such corporations to make a profit for their executives and shareholders rather than plowing that money back into America's chronically underfunded public education system.

Meanwhile, according to the *New York Times*, the junk bond specialist Michael Milken is in the process of building what he calls "the preeminent for profit education and training company in the world" through "seeking business opportunities that involve learning at every stage of life." Milken's Knowledge Learning Corporation now runs some 2,000 day-care centers, an online K–12 curriculum company, and after-school and tutoring programs, and he "hopes to be an outsourcing partner to the public school system."[42]

The Ultimate Dangers of Vouchers and Privatization

The combined threat of vouchers and privatization goes far beyond the morally questionable practice of corporations making money out of the education of this country's children and young people. Since no proposed or presently installed voucher or tuition tax credit plan has ever provided sufficient money to cover the full cost of most non–public school tuitions, those private options would almost certainly be available largely if not entirely to parents prosperous enough to make up the difference on their own. Parents and children, mostly poor and minority, who would be unable to do so would have to continue to use the public schools, which could then become schools for only—or at least primarily—those poor and minority children. The result of any such happening would be the exacerbation of what we already have—two separate and unequal American school systems based on social class. If the privatizers have their way, what we could all too easily end up with is a well-funded private and often for-profit system for the relatively well-off and predominantly middle-class Whites and members of minority groups, and a poorly supported public one serving primarily poor White and poor minority children.

While voters in several states have soundly rejected voucher proposals, and while Congress has so far resolutely resisted this privatization approach of both vouchers and tuition tax credits at the federal level, the U.S. Supreme Court has allowed the use of vouchers at some state and local levels, including for religious schools, and has not ruled out fully allowing them.

The Final Nails in the Progressive Coffin

Although the overt movement to privatize the public schools through vouchers and tax credits has so far been allowed to advance only gradually, this has not slowed the massive and continuing assault on the public schools and the attempts to eliminate any lingering traces of progressivism.

Indeed, NCLB signals the completed success of the autocratic, antiprogressive, industrialized, "machine in the mind" system of public education. It is the full realization of Taylor's corporate/industrial model and Cubberley's "schools as factories with children as raw material fed into the system to be shaped and fashioned into usable products with the specifications for manufacturing coming from the demands of twenty first century civilization, (i.e., the corporate world) with the business of the school being to build its pupils to the specifications laid down. This, of course, demands the continuous measurement of production to see if it is according to specifications." Thus NCLB's reliance on endless standardized testing, on teaching to those tests, and often on the use of standardized "scripts" for teachers slavishly to follow in their teaching. None of these practices could, as we shall see in the following chapter, be less in line with what we are beginning to know about how children and young people actually go about the task of learning about and understanding the world they will be living in as adult citizens.

CHAPTER 5

Development as the Aim of Education

If we are to create that system of developmentally based education that is humane, educationally effective, and truly democratic, we will need to base that system on Alison Gopnik's "science of children's minds." The practitioners of traditional formal schooling throughout Western history, says Gopnik, have assumed that if children had any innate mental characteristics at all, these were characteristics of "passion rather than reason, instinct rather than intellect." Their minds were essentially blank slates, empty vessels that needed to be filled with all the established orthodox social values and academic knowledge and skills, so that the children could become "rational, knowledgeable, civilized adults."

Although many thinkers throughout Western history have speculated about what goes on in children's minds, says Gopnik, no one scientifically studied children until the 1930s. "That first empirical research," she says, "by Jean Piaget and Lev Vygotsky reversed the traditional view" of empty children's minds. "Piaget concluded that even very young children spontaneously and actively reasoned about the world. Vygotsky concluded that adults naturally and spontaneously did things that helped children to reason about the world."

In the 1960s, says Gopnik, Piaget and Vygotsky were rediscovered as part of the new discipline of cognitive science. "From the findings of that science," she says, many developmental psychologists now believe that:

> our everyday behavior, the way [children] naturally see, speak, think, and act depends on abstract and complex kinds of knowledge, including knowledge of how the natural world works and of the intentions of other people. . . . As a result, we have learned more about what children know and how they learn in the last thirty years then we did in the preceding two thousand years.

For instance, she goes on to say, children have some innate knowledge of other people.

> Infants already seem to know that other people have feelings that are like their own, but children also learn a great deal about minds. Before they are three years

old, they have learned that, in addition to having feelings, people have percep-
tions and desires. By the time they reach school, they have also learned that other
people have thoughts that may differ from their own thoughts.

By the time children are ready to go to school, Gopnik says, they have
learned that different people may interpret information in different ways (but
not that such differences are necessarily legitimate) and that other people have
different personalities. Other people in the everyday world also help children
learn these things without necessarily any intention of "instructing" them. The
way that parents, and especially older siblings, talk about thoughts and feelings seems to influence children's ideas about the mind.

Additionally, children learn about everyday (and most often inaccurate)
biology and physics in much the same way they learn everyday psychology
and their native language. Even when they are in school, they continue
spontaneously to develop new ideas about how weight and size are related
and what makes things alive, whether these things are in the school's formal
curriculum or not. Children also spontaneously learn about language, numbers, and music.

Yes, Gopnik goes on to say, children appear to be endowed with innate
knowledge (such as the innate knowledge of other people), but the new research shows that the child's ability to learn is even more remarkable.

> When we study children over time, we see a succession of related pictures of the
> world. Each new picture builds on the child's earlier ideas, but also revises those
> ideas in the light of new experiences. . . . Children reshape their representations
> of the world [or what we have here been calling their "models" of the world] as
> they explore, experiment and learn. They actively seek out evidence that is rele-
> vant to the problems they face, and they actively try to construct coherent ex-
> planations of that new evidence.

Indeed, Gopnik says, some (but not all) developmental psychologists
believe that children develop knowledge in a way similar to the way scientists
conduct the enterprise of science. "Children seem to construct successive theories [models] of the world that are the product of both their earlier theories
and new evidence."[43]

Murray Gell-Mann once again puts in a cogent note here when he says:
"As we know, there is not really such a thing as education. There is only helping somebody to learn, and the learning process is a complex adaptive system;
fooling around, making mistakes, somehow having contact with reality or truth,
correcting the mistakes, assuring self-consistency and so on"—in short, "messing about."[44]

This new developmental cognitive science, in Gopnik's view, raises profound questions for educators.

If children are so smart by nature, why do so many of them seem so stupid in the classroom? The research shows that most children spontaneously learn and that most adults spontaneously help them learn. But when we explicitly set out to teach children we often fail dismally. Why can't we harness their capacities in the institutions we call schools?

Gopnik's answer is that "the interactions between children and adults that seem so important in everyday learning are very different from the usual classroom interactions." In a typical classroom, she says, children are rarely asked to use their innate capabilities for constructing complex kinds of knowledge. They "rarely get to formulate a theory, make a prediction, or construct an explanation. Children hear something about science, but they almost never actually do science."

> Imagine if we taught baseball the way we teach science [or, one might add, the way we teach anything at all]. Until they were twelve, children would read about baseball technique and occasionally hear inspirational stories of the great baseball players. They would answer quizzes about baseball rules. Conservative coaches would argue that we ought to make children practice fundamental baseball skills, throwing the ball to second base twenty times in a row, followed by tagging first base seventy times. Others would reply that the economic history of the reserve clause proved that there was, in fact, no such thing as "objectively accurate" pitching. Undergraduates might be allowed, under strict supervision, to reproduce famous historic baseball plays. But only in graduate school would they, at last, get to play a game. If we taught baseball this way, we might expect the same degree of success in the Little League World Series that we currently see in [educational] performance.[45]

The Concept of Multiple Intelligences

Howard Gardner, in his 1985 book, *Frames of Mind: The Theory of Multiple Intelligences,* and in many subsequent volumes, expands on these ideas about how children learn. He sees what we call "intelligence" not as a single entity but as consisting of "multiple" cognitive capacities or intelligences (he suggests that there are at least eight) that are interactive and interdependent:

- Spatial/visual: the ability to think, communicate, perform tasks, and solve problems involving visual skills. This would include such practical skills as recognizing edible and nonedible food, recognizing friends and predators, inventing new tools and technologies, and so on. Later it will also develop the communication systems of the visual arts such as reading, writing, painting, sculpture, and architecture.

- Kinetic: the ability to think, communicate, detect, and solve problems through the use of the body and bodily motion. This would include such practical, everyday Great Progenitor motor skills as upright walking, running, food gathering and scavenging, emotional gesturing and all forms of body language, grooming, physical play, defense, and combat, and so on. Later on it also includes very importantly the dance and organized sports.
- Musical: the ability to think, communicate, perform tasks, and eventually create works of art (including music to accompany the dance) using the human voice, musical instruments, and much later, musical notation. Some scholars are also suggesting that the human capacity for speech eventually evolved from this earlier capacity for song.
- Personal: the ability to be conscious of oneself, understand oneself, and use this self-knowledge in productive ways, including artistic creation.
- Social/interpersonal: the ability to be conscious of, relate to, and be skillful at understanding other people. This would include all social, political, and managerial skills.
- Naturalistic: the capacity for noticing, understanding, and making use of the workings of the natural world, a form of intelligence that would have considerable survival and therefore evolutionary value for a species as physically weak and vulnerable as our ancestors—and ourselves.
- Verbal: The capacity to acquire and use a culturally determined human language to speak and thus communicate in elaborate and productive ways with other human beings through both verbal exchange and eventually the written word.
- Logico-mathematical: the capacity to think logically, to grasp the concept of number, and eventually to build systems of complex thought.[46]

Gardner believes that any responsible, truly effective, and democratic educational system must assist all children in developing all these intellectual capacities and that all children can do so if they are treated to a courteous (i.e., appropriate, suitable, fitting) educational environment:

> All cognitive abilities exist in all human beings, needing only the proper circumstances or motivation to be elicited. . . . And yet . . . a pervasive antagonism often develops between the school's logical, out-of-context knowledge system and that practical participation in daily activities fostered informally by the culture. If this antagonism is to be lessened, schools . . . must be designed and viewed as comfortable and significant environments, rather than hostile providers of useless knowledge. This means that schools must contain everyday life within their walls and must make clear the relation between the skills they teach and the problems children find significant.[47]

As Gardner has also noted:

> The single most important contribution education can make to a child's development is to help him [or her] toward a field where his talents best suit him [or her], where he [or she] will be satisfied and competent. We've completely lost sight of that. Instead, we subject everyone to an education where, if you succeed, you will be best suited to be a college professor. And we evaluate everyone according to whether they meet that narrow standard of success.
>
> We should spend less time ranking children and more time helping them to identify their natural competencies and gifts and cultivate those. There are hundreds and hundreds of ways to succeed and many, many different abilities that will help you get there.[48]

So it would appear that many cognitive scientists are calling for precisely the developmental educational system that we have been attempting to outline here. Cognitive science, in short, is telling us that the great progressive educators, even if they may not yet have had the empirical scientific evidence to support their ideas, were very much on the rightest of tracks.

If that is the case, if we want to create an educational system that is based upon what we now believe science tells us about how children learn, if we want a system that capitalizes on the fact that "children are smart by nature" and makes it difficult if not impossible for our children and young people to be "stupid in the classroom," then we will have to build a system that is radically different from the one we have now.

Helping Children to Make Sense of the World

We are therefore also in territory mapped out for us by Vygotsky, with his insistence that rather than concentrating solely on the purely academic progress of the individual child we should be looking at the social nature of learning and the social prerequisites for the total cognitive development of our children and young people.

Vygotsky sees such human development as most effectively achieved through the establishment of a culture of collaborative learning that can take place in a wide variety of environments, even in schools, if they are properly organized and run.

Vygotsky also insisted that such a collaborative culture must include and to a large degree be based upon the practice of rule-bound play, that is, the kind of self-generated, rule-regulated activity we see in sandlot baseball and stickball games. Gardner describes this kind of Vygotskian activity as "play as rule following, play as symbolic transformation, play as an arena for experimentation with more advanced schemes." It is through such social game playing, he says, that children begin to achieve "greater mastery of the world, more adequate coping with problems and fears, superior understanding of oneself and one's relationship to the world, an initial exploration of the relations between fantasy and reality, an arena in which intuitive, semilogical forms of thought are freely tested."[49]

One way of assisting children to make this kind of Piagetian/Vygotskyan sense of the world is to make sure that the educational process employs the idea of recontextualization, of reconnecting schooling with the larger society, very much including the domestic world of home and family.

Which means that the American educational system should attempt to revive and restore in modern, greatly enriched form that great contextual university of the apprentice/mentoring system, in short, a progressive educational process that not only anchors children in the world in which they live but also helps them to engage in more complex intellectual model-building activities and gain a richer understanding of the world they will perforce inhabit as adult citizens.

Bringing the World into the School

Any such developmental educational process must help students to learn about the "real" world as much as possible from firsthand experience. One such developmental approach is based upon the unparalleled educational opportunity that the running of a school offers. As educators we need to see that the life our students are leading in their schools can become the firsthand-experience basis for a large part of the school's curriculum. Instead of always treating students as a problem that schools must somehow deal with and thereby robbing them of any genuine responsibility for their own education, we can begin to see students and their families as a major part of the solution to those problems.

One tested way to do this is to introduce into our schools the developmentally progressive principles of what is called "microsociety" schooling as set forth by the late George Richmond in his book *The Microsociety School: A Real World in Miniature.*[50] This model asks elementary and middle school students to play an elaborate, rule-bound Vygotskian game of creating in school a simulation of the "real" or nonschool society, a small version of the larger society that the complete range of students, in both elementary schools and high schools and including the "college bound," must design and run largely by themselves (thus, in Richmond's terms, a microsociety). There are now some 200 schools in this country that have adopted at least in part this educational approach.

What follows here is a description based upon an actual school, the Clement C. McDonough Microsociety City Magnet School, created in Lowell,

Massachusetts, in 1983 as the first full-time microsociety school. It was a school that ran successfully for more than 23 years, until 2005, when it was forced to close its doors and become a small part of another, essentially incompatible school, in no small measure as a result of the NCLB agenda. Both George Richmond and I had a hand in the creation and then the operation of this school throughout its 20-plus-year history.

Before its forced closure, the McDonough was a "citywide" magnet school, a school that had no neighborhood attendance area. The 360 K–8 students (with a waiting list of 150 or so students) came from all over the city. They were all volunteers—that is, their parents had taken them out of their neighborhood schools and asked that they come to this school. Students were admitted on a first-come, first-served basis, but admissions were carefully controlled under Lowell's "controlled choice" desegregation plan to make sure that poor and minority students had equal access. Thus 48% of the seats at the City School were reserved for minority students (African American, Hispanic, and Asian). If the applications by any ethnic group exceeded the number of reserved seats, a lottery was held to determine who was admitted. Lottery losers were placed on the waiting list. The student body was thus an accurate cross section of Lowell's public school population, with 70% of the students eligible for free or reduced-price lunch.

Tom Malone, the school's principal, describes the makeup of this school:

> All of our teachers were volunteers. And so was I. So, in that sense, everyone in this school—students, parents, teachers, and principal—was a volunteer and had chosen to be here because they wanted to be here.
>
> What that meant was that everyone here was in agreement that the school should be a microsociety school. There may not have been total agreement on exactly what that meant, since we were always in the process of arguing about and developing the school. We were growing and changing things every day, so there was a great deal of discussion back and forth, and that's healthy and as it should be. But it did make an enormous difference that we all had a basic agreement about what kind of school we should be. It made us able to get on with the job, with everyone participating instead of arguing about whether we should or should not have a school like this.

The City Magnet, operating as a true microsociety school, attempted to break down the disconnection between schooling and life out in the "real" world, to have its students learn that the things one can learn in school were not invented simply to torment innocent children at their school desks, but that they really do have some application to and for life as it is lived by the adult society.

But this school attempted to achieve this fundamental goal—among others—in a way that was quite different from the way most schools are organized and run. A "microsociety" school is based on the idea that the students—with the help and guidance of their teachers—have to design and run their own democratic, controlled free-market society in school.

The students at this school—with the help of the teachers, of course—set up their own government, creating their own legislative, executive, and judicial branches. They wrote (and were continually revising, amending, and updating) their own school constitution and their own school laws. They set up their own elected legislature; their own courts and system of justice; their own system of taxation through their own internal revenue service; their own City School lottery; and even their own police force, called the City School Crime Stoppers.

They also created their own school economy and their own currency—called the mogan instead of the dollar, because it was named after Patrick J. Mogan, who was superintendent of schools back in 1983, when the school was created. The students ran two banks—every student in the school had his or her own bank account with checkbooks and checks—and a whole slew of businesses, including law firms; corporations that manufacture and sold things; and retail enterprises that sold such items as stationery, pencils, and erasers. The curriculum also had a thriving publishing side, which essentially constituted the school's language arts program. Students wrote, edited, and desktop-published their own newspapers, books, literary magazines, and yearbooks.

All these activities were real jobs—everyone was paid for doing all these things; everyone had to have and hold at least one job in the microsociety (and students often held several jobs simultaneously) and earn his or her own keep, just as most people do in real life. One of the school's metaphorical mottoes was "In this school, there's no free lunch" (this motto being metaphorical because the less well-off students in the school actually did get a free or reduced-price lunch).

To learn all the things a student needed to learn in order to earn a living and participate in the school society, they not only learned on the job in the context of in their small society, but they also had to "go to school" to make sure that they acquired all the competencies they needed in order to succeed and hold high-level and rewarding jobs. Thus the school operated a school within a school, called the City School Academy. These were the more or less regular classes that were conducted during most of the morning hours in each of the school's major curricular strands—publishing (language arts), economy (math and economics), citizenship/government (history and social studies) and science/high tech (where students learned to use computers and software in the context of all their other strands and to use the school's building itself and all downtown Lowell as their science and environmental laboratories).

But these classes weren't free—every student had to pay tuition out of the money he or she earned through holding jobs in the rest of the microsociety. These classes (and the necessary tuition payments) were required of all students, up to the point of passing the placement exams at the highest level.

These "placement" (originally called "competency") exams were basically diagnostic tests established by the teachers that every student had to take to determine—in conjunction with the student's actual performance in the microsociety world of real jobs—how far the student was along the road to full competency in each of the school's strands. A student's performance on these exams plus his or her demonstrated level of competence in the workplace, which together constituted the school's "educational standards," determined the level of the job that he or she was able to hold in the school's society and also made up the major part of the school's assessment and accountability design.

For instance, in order to get a full-fledged job in a bank or start a business, students had to work as apprentices in those existing institutions until they achieved specified levels of competency on the banking and accounting exams, thus exhibiting a mastery of both the mathematics and the economics involved. To get a full-fledged job on a newspaper or a magazine, a student had to pass the publishing exam at an acceptable still level in reading, writing, and journalism. To become a lawyer or a judge in the judicial system, a student had to pass the bar exam.

What is most important here is how different this "placement" test system was from the conventional standardized test procedures and thus how they constituted a more educationally productive "assessment" system. In the conventional system, students are prepared for a test by repeatedly going over the material and skills they will be tested on and even practicing test taking on the past year's tests. For the student, there is no intrinsic reason for taking the test other than to pass it. The reward for passing a test is simply the small satisfaction of passing it, the external reward of being promoted to the following grade, or both.

Under the placement system, the reason for taking the test was intrinsically clear: to get a more rewarding (and better-paying) job and the advanced and more challenging activities the new job would make possible. The "passing" of the bar exam, for instance, would be based not only on the pencil-and-paper exam but also on the student's demonstrated knowledge and skills as an apprentice in a law firm or as a court employee. All this, of course, reflecting what actually goes on in that "real" world outside school.

These exams also served as part of the school's graduation requirements. Students were expected to perform with reasonable competence on all the major strand exams along with demonstrated success in the on-the-job activities and success in the role of a citizen of the school society. Thus before students graduated from this school, they had to demonstrate that they had acquired not only all their "basic" skills in reading, writing, and arithmetic, but a great deal more besides, including the knowledge of what makes a democratic human society, based upon laws rather than men and women, work.

As Richmond has described this process, the microsociety school is "a living experiment" in the development and application of each student's intellectual, social, political, and especially moral powers, the construction of those more complex and sophisticated mental models and nurturing capacities that the great progressive educators hoped children and young people would acquire.

Both the students and the adults in a microsociety school, says Richmond,

> constantly face moral dilemmas that they must solve as they strive to build a "good" society. Do you want a micro-society with the extremes of poverty and wealth? Do you want a state based on law or one based on fear and violence? Should the micro-society's government assist or ignore children who may not be succeeding? Do you want a democracy or a totalitarian state? Who can be a citizen and what burdens and responsibilities should citizens shoulder? What kinds of activities should be taxed? When does one put the community's welfare ahead of the rights of the individual? What civil rights should children enjoy in their micro-society? When has justice been done?"[51]

Tom Malone was one of the original teachers when this school was created. He comments:

> I think that there are two main reasons why we considered this to be a successful school. One was the microsociety itself, the fact that we offered an unusual curriculum that actually works. We did surveys of our parents, and a lot of them mentioned the microsociety curriculum as the main attraction, including parents who do expect that their children will go on to college. They did see it as a school that really does prepare kids for life. Many of our parents were working-class people who were very concerned with their kids making it and being successful in the world of work. And many of our parents came into the school and helped the kids learn about what they did out in their working lives—including doctors, lawyers, bankers, and the like. . . .
>
> And I firmly believe that the microsociety made a real contribution to our kids learning all the basic skills—they simply couldn't survive in this small society unless they buckled down and learned and passed those exams, unless they became competent at the jobs they went on to perform. Otherwise you went on our equivalent of welfare, and kids here hated doing that. And our test scores showed that kids here did learn all their basic skills—and I think they learned them better than they would in a regular school. Although the standardized tests we were forced to give showed us a little behind the national averages in reading, our kids were a year ahead of the national norms in math.
>
> But I also firmly believe that this school conveyed a very strong message to every kid saying that in this society everyone cares deeply

about everyone else. Every kid learned either very quickly or certainly after being here for a very short time that if this society was going to work, everyone had to pitch in and help each other, that in fact no society works unless everyone cares enough about everyone else enough to make it work.

The legislature was one way this happened, but we had a lot of other ways whereby kids simply and spontaneously helped each other. We had volunteer tutoring programs, and every day we saw kids making sure that other kids were being treated decently and that they were succeeding, even in cases where a kid may have been quite convinced he or she couldn't succeed.

And speaking of success—and not just in terms of economic success—there was the case of Eddie Gonzalez, a shy eighth-grade boy not considered by the school's staff as likely to be one of the school's stars. Indeed, because of his low academic test scores he was thought of as being a marginal student at best and at worst a potential dropout.

Enter Henry Richard, the school's industrial arts teacher. Henry had the idea that his students—both male and female—might just possibly be interested in building and then actually racing model cars powered by the carbon dioxide cartridges used for seltzer bottles—or "CO_2 cars," as they quickly came to be called.

One of the students the idea particularly appealed to was Eddie Gonzalez. Eddie had been a partner in a previous microsociety business, but that hadn't gone well, so he did not want any partners in any new business he might start. Which meant that he first had to overcome the terror of undertaking a complex business venture completely on his own.

So he settled down and began to study Henry Richard's design material on how to build a CO_2 car—how to acquire the right material, how to design cars that would have competitive speeds, what tools would be needed to manufacture them, what each car might cost, and what he would have to charge prospective customers—in short, the whole ball of research/development/engineering/business wax. Including where he was going to raise the money to front-end the entire Gonzales Motor Company's industrial empire.

Starting a business at City Magnet was not a simple enterprise. First, a clear description of the item to be manufactured had to be prepared and submitted to the executive branch's patent office. If approved, the patent gave the entrepreneur exclusive rights to manufacture the item. Armed with the patent, the prospective businessperson was now in a position to draw up his or her financing plan, explaining precisely how the item would be manufactured, who would manufacture it (the business's staff and payroll), how much would be charged for each item, any advertising costs, and so on. This plan was then taken to the business-loan officer at one or both of the school's banks so a business loan could be applied for.

Eddie Gonzalez went through all the first steps with flying colors—until he got to the banking part. He had never taken out a loan before and was scared that he might not be able to repay it. But he managed somehow to conquer that fear. He applied for and got an 8,000-mogan loan, a huge loan by microsociety standards. So he began.

He hired his workers and "cross-trained" them to perform all the tasks involved in producing and selling CO_2 cars, including sales, product fabrication, and bookkeeping. He rented store space in the school's marketplace as his retail outlet to sell the cars. He announced that there would be (and he set a date for) the big CO_2 car race. He advertised his wares in the school's two newspapers, hired CMS TV, the school's video news department, to cover and tape the event and hired Confection Connection, the school's restaurant operation, to cater the race.

But there were problems, most of them stemming from the booming success of the Gonzales automotive empire. He suddenly found himself with a 2-month backlog of orders and had to hire and train additional workers, not all of whom turned out to be totally reliable and hardworking.

But he and other people in the school were also realizing the positive ripple effects that his success was having on the rest of the school and its economy. In addition to hiring the TV and catering outfits and thus helping them to be successful, he took out ads in the school's newspapers, thus adding to their income. And, of course, he and his business and its employees were all able to pay their full share of taxes, thus enriching the school government's treasury.

Further, when Race Day finally came and was held in the school's gym, it was one of the school's biggest and most successful events, including a great deal of sub-rosa betting (contextual mathematics) on individual cars and races, even though gambling was officially proscribed.

As for Eddie himself, he progressed from being that shy, "low self-esteem" kid no one thought much of to a citizen who overcame all his initial fears, who discovered the importance of all the "basic" skills he had learned and the importance of teamwork, who learned to "wheel and deal" in making business decisions, and who discovered as well the positive effects his efforts had on the entire school.

The Founding Principle of Microsociety Schooling

The intellectual foundation for any school's microsociety curriculum is the school's constitution. The first and perhaps most crucial step in creating microsociety schooling involves requiring students to take some genuine responsibility for their own educational lives by giving them as the governed a large degree of consensual power in school decisions and in the everyday work of keeping the institution running. And it is also a way of solving many of those seemingly intractable problems of discipline and danger.

At the very beginning of this process is the constitutional activity that involves the students in exploring and hopefully grasping the great principle of reciprocity that makes a democratic society—or any society, for that matter—actually work. Everything the students do in this kind of school involves the cooperative efforts of the students themselves, as they replay in their school the collaborative cultural process by which we evolved into human beings in the first place. To start a microsociety school, the entire school community, every student and all adults, must become involved in writing that school constitution, most often using the 1787 Constitutional Convention in Philadelphia as a general model.

The students in each class, from kindergarten on up (coached, but not "instructed," by their teachers) must spend the first few weeks—at least a full month in most cases—developing some preliminary answers to a set of fundamental constitutional questions, using (if they choose) the U.S. Constitution as a guide but not necessarily as a document to be slavishly imitated. Indeed, one of the first things the City School students discovered and were appalled by when they originally tackled the constitutional process was that the 1787 version of the Constitution did not contain a bill of rights. They made very sure that their constitution did. (Although kindergarten and primary-level students can and do take part in this process and do remarkably well in it, the process works most powerfully from about third grade up).

Some of the fundamental constitutional questions the students wrestled with were the following:

- What are the different kinds of societies that have existed in the world up to now? What do we mean when we say that we in this country live in a "democratic" society? What kind of society do we want to have in this school? (In most cases of microsociety schooling, the students have decided that their society should be a representative democratic society, although one school did choose to have a constitutional and therefore democratic monarchy).
- What then does it mean to be a "citizen" of a democratic society? Who can be a citizen? All kids? Can teachers be citizens? What about parents?
- What are the rights and responsibilities of a citizen of this school society? How do we define what a "right" is and what a "responsibility" is?
- What is a "law" and how do laws get to be laws? Do we want laws in our school society? If so, what should they be?

- If we have laws, how do we make sure that the citizens of this school will follow and obey those laws?
- How do we want our school society to work? What kinds of governmental structures will we need if our society is to work?

Once all the classes have gravely considered these questions and come up with a raft of tentative and often wildly conflicting answers, including children writing out (and then defending) their ideas about what a "good" society might and should be, each class must then elect at least one delegate and one alternate delegate to the school's Constitutional Convention. The delegates all bring with them the results of the class discussions. It is now their job—again using the Philadelphia convention as a rough guide—to begin to build the school's actual constitution using what the classes have come up with as the initial material for discussion.

At the end of each daily convention session (usually held in the mornings), the delegates must return to their home classes and report on what has transpired at the convention—what has been discussed and what, if anything, has been tentatively decided. The class then reviews what has transpired and voices any and all objections and recommendations. The delegates must take these complaints and suggestions back to the convention's following session.

This part of the exercise is crucial, since each class (acting as each of the 13 colonies originally acted) must at the end of the convention process either ratify or reject the final document. If ratified, the constitution becomes the consensual agreement, the social contract, by which everyone in the school, child and adult, is expected to conduct themselves. Once the constitution is written, the opening days of each school year are spent in a new constitutional convention, reviewing the document and seeing if any changes or amendments are needed.

In the writing of their constitutions, the students in most microsociety instances have created an elected (and usually unicameral) student-run legislature with the power to make and enforce school laws; an executive branch with an president and vice president (elected only after a vigorous and often contentious electoral process) and its very own bureaucracy to operate the government offices (including an internal revenue service to collect the taxes); a system of school justice with a police department and courts; an operating economy with its own currency, banks, corporations, and markets; an elaborate computer-based publishing industry putting out newspapers, magazines, and books; and a science/high-technology strand concentrating on setting up sophisticated computer systems for the banks and businesses and for desktop publishing programs for the publishing ventures while also using the school building itself and its surroundings as an environmental laboratory.

The activities involved in doing all these things and making sure that they can continue to be done—including thinking long and hard about whether it is all work in the way it is supposed to work (and if not what might be done about it)—constitutes the fundamental set of ideas upon which the school's "curriculum" is based.

For instance, if weapons and student violence or sexual harassment are problems, it is now up to the school's designated and elected legislature and executive branch to construct a solution to such problems. After all, it is the students themselves who are most aware of and are most victimized by the usually, small band of thugs who have the knives and guns or the small band of sexual harassers.

But in the traditional school situation the terrorized majority of students is rarely helped to do what any human society must do in such a situation, which is to organize itself and create institutions such as a student-run system of school justice, encompassing a police force and court system, that is specifically created first to establish and then maintain domestic (or in this case school) tranquility through the control of violence and the protection of its citizens.

This minimally means that the students themselves have to devise their own constitutionally established system of social rules and regulations that ensures that armed schoolmates are disarmed; that there are both civil and criminal mechanisms for resolving crimes such as theft, sexual harassment, and disputes between students; and that there are ways in which the democratically arrived-at decrees of the system can be enforced.

In a similar fashion, students could and should become responsible (with guidance provided by adults) for and care about their entire physical environment, including assisting in the task of keeping the building clean and in good repair. And both males and females might even become responsible for such things as the quality and preparation and serving of food in a civilized, non–zoo cafeteria environment. They might, for instance, help to set up and run the cafeteria as a restaurant business with all the amenities and rules of civilized behavior that would apply in a real restaurant. As David Cronin, one of the school's original teachers, once put it, "I don't care where a kid is or what he's doing as long as he's using his mind." Malone remarks:

> One thing that was very interesting about this school, I think is that in many ways it was not simply a replication of that "real" world out there. It was in many ways a better, a much more caring society, a sort of idealized version of what that "real" world might be. For instance, in this society, which was racially, ethnically, and economically an almost perfect mirror of Lowell itself, most of the important governmental and economic positions—president, legislature, business entrepreneurs, and so on—were held by young women, and minority young women at that. Which, I can assure you, is not the situation in the real world of Lowell, Massachusetts.

And in this school every kid had the full powers of citizenship and could realistically aspire to any position in the society he or she wanted to attain and was willing to work for. And it didn't seem to matter what social or economic class a student came from. In fact, one of our hopes here was that having experienced what a considerably more just, caring, and genuinely democratic society is like, insofar as we could help them create that society here, the students would be less willing to go along with the inequities, injustices, and the callousness of that "real" world out there as they grow up and have to deal with that world.

The Vision of a Perfect, Complete Microsociety School

Now, although Lowell's City Microsociety School was very much a splendid pioneering step in at least one developmental direction, it never became what I imagined as a total or complete microsociety school.

For instance, alert readers here will have noticed that there is a missing piece in the description of this microsociety school, an omission that violates one of the fundamental rules of developmental schooling—that education should begin not only with and be richly concerned with our concrete technologies but also very much with all the humanities and the fine and performing arts.

While the City School did deal in many ways with a broad variety of human endeavors, there was no separate curricular strand for the fine and performing arts. This omission can be explained, if not excused, by the fact that when the parent choice surveys were conducted in Lowell the two most desired schools were the microsociety and a school for the fine and performing arts. Both these schools were created, and they shared the rehabilitated building that was specifically designed for each school's special program. The idea was that they would collaborate—share programs and activities—and thus essentially become a single school. Unfortunately, the Arts School was badly mismanaged and was eventually abandoned, so such collaborations never materialized.

But most important, the bulk of the school day at City Magnet was still taken up primarily with academy classes, with only 1 or 2 hours a day devoted to the actual microactivities of operating the in-school society. While the teaching that went on in the academy classes was almost always intimately tied into the microactivity experiences, it was those microactivities that constituted the school's "real world," "in-context" experiences for the students. These activities were also the part of the school day that the students clearly most enjoyed and appreciated, the time when they felt they were most in touch with and experiencing what the "real world" would actually be like when they become adults.

Indeed, given the experiences we had at the City Magnet for more than 20 years and given an opportunity to start a new such school, I would now lobby long and hard for a reversal of the City Magnet's approach. I would make the microactivities the basic operating mode of the school, with academy classes always available but primarily used when, and if, the students (and their teachers) felt the need for them to make their school society operate in a better, more productive, and certainly more humane fashion. After all, it clearly makes more sense to learn how to add, subtract, multiply, and divide through keeping and balancing your own checking account or actually working in the school's bank and having a teacher or other more advanced students teaching you these things in context than to attempt to learn those skills in a decontexualized classroom.

The School/Community Learning Center

And speaking of physical facilities, what all forms of developmental schooling clearly require is a radically different approach not only to the process of schooling but also to what we conventionally think of as a "school" building. In that conventional picture, an educational facility is set off by itself and typically surrounded by playing fields—the classic educational ghetto described earlier.

For elementary schools, such a facility will minimally house in one or more individual buildings a series of 800 square foot classrooms; an administrative office; a gym; if one is lucky, a library; a computer lab; and an auditorium. The secondary school version will add to these basic spaces science labs, perhaps music and art spaces, and perhaps a swimming pool.

So—thinking now in strictly ideal and possibly utopian terms—the first requirement set forth by any developmental schooling process is that we abolish "school" as an educational ghetto and replace it with a new animal that might be called a school/community learning center, that is, a facility that is not cut off from its surrounding community but rather is centrally located and mixed in with that community.

It should to the greatest extent possible be located adjacent to or within easy walking distance of libraries, city hall and other government agencies, cultural institutions, shopping centers, businesses, and parks (for sports, horticulture, recreation), all of which will become part of the school's curriculum. These facilities could even be "joint occupancies"—school, community, and private institutions sharing one physical building.

A second requirement is that such a facility should actually contain within itself spaces for community resource and family services directly related to the school's own educational mission: a family center and spaces for day care, family medical, welfare, and social service agencies. All these agencies would share in the cost of building the building and operating the center's collaborative program.

A third set of requirements completely alters the conventional "instructional" arrangements and their associated spaces, based on the fundamental necessity to found formal schooling on Gardner's first six intelligences while interweaving these with the verbal and logico-mathematical capacities. There will be spaces for the fine and performing arts, such as theaters, art rooms, dance studios, fully equipped music practice rooms and listening rooms equipped with hi-fi surround-sound machines, and ceramic studios with kilns; botanical (horticultural and agricultural) spaces, both indoor and outdoor, for growing all sorts of plants and food crops, that is, greenhouses, outdoor plots for vegetables and other food plants (grown for and served in the student-run restaurant/cafeteria), labs for grafting and hybridization, and animal husbandry spaces for raising and caring for small animals such as mice, gerbils, and rabbits. There should also be technological workshop spaces, including mechanical, woodworking, and engineering design and execution shops.

For microsociety schools there need to be specialized spaces for the school government: legislative chamber(s); executive-branch offices (for the school president, vice president, internal revenue, police, patent office, and personnel, among others); areas for the judicial system (courtrooms, judge's chambers, legal offices). There also need to be curricular-strand spaces (in addition to fine and performing arts spaces): publishing offices (for newspapers, magazines, and books); TV, radio, and film studios; economy spaces (banks, marketplace, and manufacturing rooms); science and tech spaces (a computer resource center in addition to computers in all other facilities to be used for such activities as desktop publishing); an electronic library; and science labs (environmental, ecology, biology, physics, astronomy, weather).

There will still be a need for a small number of developmental learning spaces (formerly called classrooms) that are available for seminars, tutorials, and individual and group research projects.

And finally there should be professional office space for teachers and other adult personnel, namely, individual offices for the teaching staff, a professional resource and library center, and professional development seminar and meeting rooms, all fully equipped with telephones, computers, and other items— all the professional amenities, in short, accorded doctors, lawyers, investment bankers, industrial managers, and CEOs in the other professional ranks.

Moving School out into the World

Although we do not as yet have a high school version of a true microsociety school, we have had over the years a few sterling examples of collaboration between high schools and the real world—vocational schools, work study, cooperative education, school-to-work programs, and the like.

In almost every case, however, these are thought of as being for those "vocational" track students who are seen as not capable of going on to college (or who do not choose to go on to college) but who instead will immediately upon graduation go into the job market—if they can find a job. These students are presumably taught the skills necessary for the vitally important trades and occupations of plumbing, electrical, sheet metal, auto mechanics, food service, clerical, and so on.

We also have a few examples of real-world learning not designed as vocational education but as a different way of going to school for all students. Beginning 40 years ago with Philadelphia's Parkway Program and Chicago's Metro High School, we have had the "school without walls" concept in which students actually do "go to school" out in the larger society—in museums and other cultural institutions, at businesses, and city hall. Rochester, New York, has such a school, as does New York City in its City as School program.

Additionally, there has been of late a great deal of interest in the idea of "service learning"—students actually going out into the real world to help out in day care centers, homes for the elderly, and community organizations. In some cases, students even receive academic credit for these activities. But usually they are simply add-ons to the academic curriculum and not considered part of the core of secondary education.

These have all been important steps forward, but they are small steps. Instead of moving rapidly in this direction, we have kept most of our secondary students cooped up in the juvenile educational ghetto of the traditional American middle or high school. Then, when our students are at age 16, 17, or 18, we say good-bye to our dropouts, ship some of the remaining nondropouts off to a postjuvenile but still adolescent educational ghetto called college, or we release them into the adult world of work for which most of them (even after college) are only (as I was) minimally prepared, a world that looks upon them with great and possibly justified suspicion, viewing them as being ignorant, unskilled, and unready to assume adult duties and responsibilities.

What we still do not have is a large, comprehensive example of real-world, in-context learning designed to provide all high school students (very much including the college bound) with a firsthand knowledge of how the world works and what human society is all about, examples in which the educational process is jointly and collaboratively planned and conducted by the school world and the real world.

We do not, in short, have what would amount to a modernized and greatly expanded version of the extraordinarily effective in-context apprentice/mentor educational system and knowledge business that made us the human beings we are today and which was responsible for the education of most of our young people before we developed our institutions of formal disconnected lower and higher education.

We need to develop a new kind of secondary system that is an extension of the microsociety approach and thus both allows and encourages all our high school students to become the active moral, social, and political philosophers— and thus possibly the builders of that more caring, benevolent human culture— we would like to see them become.

One Possible Way to Do It

In 1972, the city of Boston and its Redevelopment Authority in collabo- ration with the Boston school system designed such a K–12 option as part of the planning for the Boston bicentennial celebration of 1975–1976. The idea was to develop a way in which public education could be a major part of that celebration. I was the leader of the team responsible for this planning.[52]

Building on the experiences of the Parkway Program and its ilk, we de- signed a program called the City as Educator (CAE) with the aim of eventu- ally serving some 20,000 elementary through Grade 12 students. It was also carefully designed to be a racially integrated experience, thus contributing to the solution of Boston's desegregation problems.

Roughly a year was spent working out how the city's schools and all it's arts and cultural institutions; its science and technology resources; its chari- table, civic, and governmental agencies; and its business and industry sector and all the area's colleges and universities could be woven into a collaborative network that would allow large numbers of public school children and young people actually to receive at least half their education by actually "going to school" in all the city's vast array of potentially educational institutions.

This required the creation of an elaborate system of joint planning involv- ing the school system, the private- and public-sector host institutions, and the city authority responsible for building schools, a system aimed at creating a new (or rather re-creating that very old contextual) approach to educating children and young people and a completely different approach to the use of school staff and school facilities.

This new system required, first, that those private- and public-sector in- stitutions not only be brought into the planning but also agree to become part of the final design. The range of institutions included the Boston Museum of Fine Arts; the Children's Museum; the Institute of Contemporary Art; the Boston Symphony; the Boston Ballet; the Boston Opera Company; the Bos- ton Public Library and all its branches; the New England Conservatory of Music; the city's local theater companies; the Franklin Park Zoo; the Massachusetts Horticultural Society; the Museum of Science; the Museum of Transportation;

the New England Aquarium; the Animal Rescue League; the Massachusetts Audubon Society; the Arnold Arboretum; Logan Airport; Massachusetts General Hospital; Harvard's Museum of Comparative Zoology and Smithsonian Observatory; Boston's city hall; the police department and local courts; the state legislature; the local gas, electric, and telephone companies; the Boston Bar Association and some of the larger law firms; the county, state, and federal court systems; the Federal Reserve Bank and the major local banks; the John Hancock and Prudential insurance companies; the Polaroid and Honeywell corporations; the Boston Redevelopment Authority itself; Harvard University; the Massachusetts Institute of Technology; Boston University; and the University of Massachusetts at Boston (this being a partial list of the entities that were initially proposed or were actually recruited).

In the case of those institutions that owned and operated private or public facilities (which was most of them), the idea involved their agreeing either to rent space in those buildings to the school system or to add jointly designed and jointly used space that would be paid for by a portion of those city and state funds that would normally go into the building of new conventional schools. Jointly created and jointly used "learning resource centers" would be set up in or next to most of the major cooperating institutions.

Those parents and children choosing the CAE program would be grouped together in their regular schools (or more ideally they would be assigned to their own home base CAE schools). They would "go to school" for one week in those local home base schools. Then for the following week they and their teachers would be transported to one of the racially integrated resource centers set up in the host institutions.

Each resource center would be staffed jointly by school system teachers and host institution staff. Since during any given school week, half of each CAE school's student population would be in the resource centers, only the remaining half would be in their home base schools. This would mean that roughly only half the normal space would be needed at the home base school, thus freeing up facilities money for the rental or construction of space at the resource centers.

We designers also created in rough outline form a completely new, interdisciplinary, hands-on, developmental curriculum that would allow the students using the resource centers to explore at firsthand all those real-world people and resources they would never have available to them in their conventional schools. Instead of trying to make sense of life and the world through studying about it in dreary textbooks and other second- and thirdhand "educational" materials inside their school ghettos, students would now study real animals at the zoo and the Audubon nature preserves; real trees and plants at the Arboretum; real aquatic life at the Aquarium; and real art and cultural life in the city's museums (including the Museum of Fine Arts), concert halls, and theaters; the real world of the sciences at the Museum of Science and in college and university laboratories; the real world of business and industry in the banks, business offices, Federal Reserve, and local industries and retail stores; the real political life of the city, state, and country at city hall, the statehouse, and the federal office buildings; the real workings of the justice system in the city's police department and its municipal, state, and federal courts; and the real operations (or nonoperations) of the transportation system at the transit authority, Logan Airport, and the city's rail stations. And so on and so on.

Needless to say, we planners did not expect any such elaborate system to be in place in the short space of 3 or 4 years and therefore by 1976. The proposal was only to develop the larger plan and have a pilot project up and running in time for the bicentennial. Even though many people in the city were quite excited by the plan, both the bicentennial and the federal court's desegregation order were scheduled to arrive at almost precisely the same moment. The agonies and disruptions involved in the desegregation crisis that did arrive in 1975 ruined any chance that the city could think or do anything about such long-range educational innovations as the City as Educator program. Instead of such thinking being incorporated into the desegregation plan, all such thought was completely destroyed and the planning was abandoned, never to be revived.

A Further Way to Do It

However, the city of Chicago in 1975 provided a way for us CAE designers further to explore and give a limited exposure to these ideas. Chicago 21 (now called Chicago United) was an alliance of many of the major private-sector institutions in the city that were intent upon building a large-scale, racially and economically mixed new community called Dearborn Park in abandoned railroad yards in the South Loop area of the city.[53]

One part of the overall plan was to develop for the new Dearborn Park community and its neighboring communities an elementary and middle school, a strictly public school educational options system based upon the idea of both parent and professional choice and of the different kinds of public schools parents wanted. It was vital that Dearborn Park's immediate neighbors be brought into this new system, since from the beginning of the development effort there was great concern on the part of everyone in the city that Dearborn Park not be seen as a wonderful, safe, walled-off, largely middle-class and predominantly White enclave separate from the rest of the city and granted special monetary and educational benefits not available to the rest of the city, and especially not to the city's low-income African American community.

In order to make sure that the educational system did include all income levels and did not either give the appearance of or in fact be a sheltered private preserve just for the children of the privileged occupants of Dearborn Park, it was decided that the predominantly poor African American inhabitants of a public housing project called Hilliard Homes to the south, the largely Hispanic inhabitants of the contiguous Pilsen neighborhood, and the inhabitants of Chinatown to the west be an integral part of the Dearborn Park system.

All parents in the four Chicago communities would be surveyed to find out what kinds of K–8 schools they wanted for their children. Given the survey results, four to five small schools (ranging from Montessori, microsociety and integrated-day schools to highly academic models) would be created, some in Dearborn Park, some in those nearby communities. All schools would have integrated student bodies through the use of controlled student assignment policies based not only on parental choice but also on the ethnic percentages of all of the children in the new four-community school district. All these small elementary schools would also have their own version of the Boston City as Educator (CAE) program, with close ties to and sharing special programs with all the nearby downtown cultural and educational institutions—the Chicago Art Institute, the Shedd Aquarium, the Adler Planetarium, the Field Natural History Museum, the Museum of Science and Industry, the Chicago Symphony, Lyric Opera, and others.

At the high school level, we planners designed a program that combined the CAE approach with a high school version of microsociety schooling. We proposed that the school system should set up small home base high schools (including one in the Dearborn Park four-community district) that carried forward to the high school level the microsociety ideas—a small society designed and run largely by the students themselves. The plan then required the creation of that network of learning resource centers housed not in any school building but—as with the CAE model—located in the city's leading business and industrial institutions, its arts and other cultural organizations, and its major public-sector institutions. These centers would be available not just to the to the Dearborn Park microsociety high school but to students from other high schools as well.

The developmental, in-context curriculum of each such center would be jointly designed and taught by public high school teachers assigned to each center by the school system and people from the particular public- or private-sector institution housing the center. Students would divide their time between the home base microsociety school and those learning centers that particularly interested them. In the learning resource centers, the students would receive their firsthand in-context experience with how the major institutions of a human society work. Back at the home base microsociety, they would pursue both the operation of their microsociety and the more reflective, critical, and theoretic model constructing activities based upon what they were directly experiencing out in the real-world learning centers. This idea was dubbed the Chicago Career Development Center Network.

The jointly developed curriculum at each center would be primarily direct, firsthand experience of the kinds of activities practiced by the host institution (for instance, studying economics by finding out how large banks, brokerage houses, large corporations, and small businesses actually work) and partly by reflecting upon that firsthand experience in classroom sessions involving the more formal study of economics taught, again jointly, by the Chicago public school teachers assigned to that center and by the experienced personnel of the host institution. Further reflective activities would also be going on back at the home base schools.

Sixteen such centers were initially planned, all in downtown Chicago, with each serving several hundred students, including a Center for Economics and Business Studies located at the First National Bank, a Center for Air Transportation Careers at Midway Airport, a Center for Communications and Computer Systems at the Illinois Bell Telephone Company, a Center for Architectural Studies at Roosevelt University, a Center for Urban Studies at the University of Illinois School of Urban Sciences, a Center for Design at the Fashion Institute of Chicago, a Center for Energy and Environmental Studies at Washburne School, a Center for Merchandising and Retailing at the Merchandise Mart, a Center for Health and Medical Careers at Rush-Presbyterian Hospital and St. Luke's Medical Center, a Center for Management Studies at Northwestern University's Kellogg School of Management, and a Center for Law and Justice at De Paul University.

Additional centers were planned to be housed in the Dearborn Park partner institutions—at the Chicago Art Institute, the Field Natural History Museum, the Museum of Industry and Technology, the Shedd Aquarium, the Chicago Symphony, the Lyric Opera, the Goodman Theater, and various other of the city's major cultural institutions but also in city hall; the Chicago Police Department; the city planning department; and other municipal, state, and federal governmental and social agencies. The idea here being to make sure that by thus broadening the network's scope well beyond anything that could be considered in any way simply vocational education, the entire program would be seen and accepted by the local colleges and universities as meeting their admissions requirements.

Two Ways to Develop Career Development Centers

When the original thinking was done for these Chicago centers, two possible ways to organize and run them were explored. The first was to make the program a citywide offering, with students (mainly juniors and seniors) from any of the city's high schools leaving their home base high schools to attend one or more of the centers part time, either every morning or every afternoon for 5 days a week or for 2 to 3 full-time days a week. This clearly required some major changes in the way those home base high schools organized and scheduled themselves—a mighty tall order, as anyone who has tried to reform an existing high school can testify. To get over this difficulty, the suggestion was made that students opting for the Career Development Center (CDC) program should be organized into a special subschool within the larger high school, a subschool that would have its own schedule, staff, and so on, making the program much more feasible.

The second way was to create additional Dearborn Park–like special new small CDC home base high schools scattered around the city, based loosely on Chicago's Parkway-like Metro High School, that would serve as the home bases for CDC students. While most of curriculum for these new schools would be conducted out in the centers, the home base would be the arena for the school's administrative, curriculum development, counseling, microsociety governance, and social activities.

In both the CDC center and home base locations, students would undertake the arduous, challenging task of reflecting upon, examining, and forming abstract rules and theories about all that firsthand experience. For it was only as a result of such a reflective process that the actual mental models being developed in their heads would be continuously constructed, deconstructed, and reconstructed and therefore gradually become increasingly complex and presumably more accurate and powerful representations of the richness and complexity of the students' external and internal worlds.

And it is through this reflective experience that the students would now call upon the thoughts, ideas, and theories, the accumulated knowledge and wisdom, of the entire human experience that is contained in all those real books, all those great works of art, and any and all other thought-provoking materials, past and present, printed or electronic, in short, all of that "content" that is normally encapsulated and denatured in our dreary textbooks and subject matter classes.

For now the students would be in a position to ask themselves—and, indeed, could hardly help but ask themselves and the world—their own very real, emotionally charged questions, engendered in their heads and hearts by what they had seen and experienced in their own families, in their local neighborhoods, and out in the larger society as well as in the social institutions they were developing and running in their microsociety home base schools: Why is it that some people are very rich and other people are very poor? Why do some people have homes and others not? Why are our cities dirty and polluted? Is this school as clean and well taken care of as it could and should be? What causes foul air and what can scientifically be done about it? What is the quality of the air and water in this school and in this city? Why do we allow guns to be manufactured and sold? What can we do about the drug-ridden, crime-ridden streets we have to walk through to get to school? Why do we have gangs? Do students still carry guns and other weapons in this school? If so, why aren't our police force and our courts working to put a halt to such activity? Do we need more police? A more effective system of punishment? Or a better way of understanding why kids bring guns to school? And while we are at it, is there anything we as students and teachers can do to make not just this school but also the community around us safer and less crime and drug ridden?

Why do bridges and buildings stand up most of the time and not fall down—and why do they sometimes fall down? Where does the food sold in the local supermarket come from? Is our drinking water safe and how might we find out if it is safe or not? Why do we put old people in nursing homes rather than keep them at home? Why do both mothers and fathers have to go out and work? How does a market economy work—and sometimes and in some ways not work at all when people are getting downsized and laid off all over the place? What is a "social safety net" and how does it work—or not work at all? Why do we have welfare and what is it like to be a welfare family? What do lawyers do? Should they be killed off as Shakespeare recommends, and we thus put them out of our misery? What could we students do right now to make the local community we live and go to school in a better, safer, more attractive place? What might we do also to make our school a better, safer, more attractive place?

How does rap music, or any kind of music, or all the different kinds of dances, plays, poetry, and stories that exist out there make life better or worse for us and for everybody in our community? What is a society of laws, not men (and presumably not women)? What do we mean when we talk of a "good" or a "just" society? Does the present American society fit such a description? Are we creating that kind of a society here in our home base school?

And so on endlessly, since there is never a dearth of questions that inevitably arise from students experiencing and thinking about what that larger world, their own school world, and their very own lives are really like. In this very real sense, we are simply continuing the richly developmental process of assisting children and young people to build those increasingly complex intellectual models and those increasingly productive habits of human nurturing first described for us by the great progressive educators.

Reconstituting Higher Education and the Knowledge Business

But in addition to all these requirements for the revitalization and renewal of our system of K–12 public schooling, we need to reshape our institutions of higher education and restore in contemporary form our two most recent (post–World War II) infusions of massive support for what the mathematician and social scientist Anatole Beck calls the human "knowledge business":

> It is an old saw that knowledge is power. [But] knowledge is also wealth, real wealth, money in the bank. It is, in fact, the realest wealth we have. . . . Each generation receives as its inheritance a vast store of knowledge, gathered over the eons. It is so pervasive that we are hardly aware of its existence, except as we are dragged, often unwillingly, through the schools and classes in which we acquire a small part of it. Also, to the extent that we are interested in that sort of thing, we might keep abreast of the inventions and innovations which are pouring almost constantly from the machinery of knowledge production the human race has created for itself. Although we are generally aware of the private inheritance of money or property we expect from our parents or other members of the older generation, we tend to be less aware of the inheritance of public property which passes constantly between generations, and most of all, we are unaware of this inheritance of accumulated knowledge and wisdom which, I maintain, is our most valuable legacy.

The general cultural and economic value of such knowledge, says Beck, can best be fully realized through an enormous investment in "what excites the curiosity of self-educated and creative people following the dictates of their own interests." And the best evidence for the predictable success of this idea, he says, is the result of the two periods in recent American history when "there was the freest rein possible given to gifted people gobbling up all the knowledge they wished to acquire."

> The first of these was the G.I. Bill which allowed the veterans of World War II [although mostly male] to be educated at public expense in whatever subject they chose with the only requirement being that be acceptable at some acceptable learning venue.
>
> The second was the "Sputnik era" of the 1960's, when excellence in education and research was widely pursued in the interests of beating the Russians to the moon and to the markets and allegiances of the Third World. We can see the profits of this open-handedness in the incredible advances of the last 40 years, already worth many times the amount of money invested and still bearing fruit.

One of Beck's most telling examples here is the invention of the silicon chip (and then the small, personal digital computer), an invention that was required and therefore created by the need for small computers for the nation's space craft. This was a very small (in money terms) investment that has had a quite literally incalculable cultural impact and an unimaginable economic return well beyond anything the original inventors could possibly have dreamed of.

This rich growth of our public knowledge business, according to Beck, has in recent years been discontinued in favor of a concentration on short-term private rewards for corporate owners and the already wealthy. Indeed, the fabulous wealth created during those 40 years has never been equally and justly distributed. Since 1970, Beck reminds us, the lower 70% of the population in this country has become poorer while the upper 30% has become richer. To many working people, the increased productivity of labor has resulted at the very least in the threat and in many cases the reality of "technological unemployment" and a significant decline in their economic power. The benefits of the growth of knowledge have not, says Beck, "trickled down" to the mass of people in the industrial world.

What the restoration of this society's GI Bill and Sputnik era fecundity, its full investment in both the private- and public-knowledge business, will require, says Beck, is an additional investment of 8 to 10% of the gross domestic product above what we are currently investing.

This would mean:

> prenatal care and nutrition, free to all, adequate nutrition and mental stimulation for all children provided from a much earlier age than now, better schools for everyone, and free college education, including room and board, to everyone who can meet the admissions standards of any accredited post-secondary institution. It will also require generous provision for graduate education, subsidized research and support of creative scientific and artistic efforts.

In short, a genuine social, political and educational revolution in contemporary American society.[54]

Any such revolution, however, will also require a radical transformation not just of our public and private systems of preschool through Grade 12 education but of our colleges and universities as well. While Beck is quite right that the GI Bill produced a remarkable opportunity for a large number of "self-educated and creative people to follow the dictates of their own interests" and "gobble up all of the knowledge they wished to acquire," this is hardly a description of the basic nature of our system of higher education or an accurate description of what happens when the vast majority of our students now enter those hallowed groves.

Since we no longer have anything resembling the GI Bill, our present system has increasingly reverted to its former model of being available primarily to those students who are somehow able to pay for it, through family subsidy, student loans, working at subsistence level jobs, or a combination of these.

In 2003 William G. Bowen, Martin A. Kurzweil, and Eugene M. Tobin reported on their study of the admissions process in 19 selective colleges and universities, including five Ivy League and five prestigious state universities.[55] What they found was that "students from families in the top income quartile were more than twice as likely as students from the bottom income quartile even to take the SAT. Among the test takers, the odds of scoring over 1200 were three times higher for those in the top quartile as compared with those in the bottom quartile. They concluded:

> Combining these probabilities, the key fact is that the odds of both taking the tests and doing very well on them were roughly six times higher for students from the top quartile than for students from the bottom quartile. Family circumstances have an enormous impact on the chances of applicants even being considered by the admissions staff at an academically selective college or university.[56]

Thus, while almost all colleges and universities now provide scholarships for "qualified" poor and minority students, exercise affirmative action in admissions, and even claim that no qualified student is ever turned down for financial reasons, this is a far cry from Beck's "free college education, including room and board, to everyone who can meet the admissions standards of any accredited postsecondary school."

While this system has broadened over the past two centuries to include technical schools, community colleges, and a host of other additions and alternatives to the classical 4-year liberal arts and sciences curriculum, it is still a system fundamentally dedicated to its historic mission of selecting and preparing students to become the educated elite that runs society. As the psychologist and evolutionary historian Merlin Donald describes them, these are those:

> educated persons who will write all the books, keep all the records, run the schools, academies and universities, control religious observances, write the history of the politics, regulate trade, produce most of the art and all of the literature and increasingly dominate the social order as a class.[57]

While it can certainly be argued that this is precisely one of the things that our colleges and universities should be there to do, it can equally be argued that this is still basically the top-down, elitist, disconnected, less than fully democratic system we have always had in the Western world. It is not a system that is based upon what University of California, Los Angeles, scholar Mike Rose calls a more "dynamic, multi-dimensional model" of intelligence,

> a conception of knowledge that doesn't separate hand from brain; that articulates the many kinds of knowing involved in work; that appreciates the interplay of the cognitive, the social, the aesthetic; that is more abundant and varied than a model built on hierarchies and binaries. In fact, a more accurate model of all the mind's work: from planning a pitched roof, to diagnosing joint pain, to the crafting of a line of poetry.[58]

It is not, in other words, a system that is carefully and deliberately designed to make full use of the intellectual capacities of the human species that Beck says is required if the human knowledge business is to realize its enormous wealth-producing potential. Indeed, as Beck reminds us, it is precisely the investment of that additional 8 to 10% of the gross domestic product that would produce the enormous growth in wealth that would more than cover the cost of that investment.

And it is in part because of the lack of Rose's "multi-dimensional model of intelligence" that we allow these institutions of "higher" learning to continue to practice their traditional, archaic form of non-Blackian, non-Ciardian, non-Morrisonian pedagogy, that process that requires its students to absorb large amounts of information presented in complex textbooks or manuals and taught by the standard collegiate model of assigned readings, lectures, and paper-and-pencil tests.

And third, it is this essentially outmoded, still limited, disconnected, hierarchical system of higher education that controls what is allowed to happen in the K–12 system that feeds it. This "higher" system compels that "lower" system to be a watered-down clone of itself, with all the conventional subject matter compartments, standardized pencil-and-paper tests, and didactic pedagogical methods. It is thus a system that effectively prevents our lower schools from being able to explore and adopt the progressive, developmental model of schooling advocated here.

I once asked Deborah Meier, the founder of the Central Park East schools, in East Harlem, what kind of schools she would run if she didn't have to worry about getting her students into conventional colleges and universities. Her answer was swift: Her schools from preschool through high school would be based upon the model of schooling carried on in good kindergartens, namely, the progressive, developmental schooling described here. And, she added, this was the model that should also be practiced by those very colleges and universities that were keeping her from running the kind of schools she believed she should be running.[59]

CHAPTER 6

Reinventing the System

If anything has so far been accomplished in this educational journey, I hope that I have at least made it clear that the present organizational structure of our Western system of education—and especially the structure of our scientifically managed, factory-model American public school system—is culturally and educationally obsolete. It is not a system equipped to promote the full range of human intelligence granted us by our evolutionary heritage and needed by our still-exploding knowledge business.

Given this present K–12 public school system with its No Child Left Behind drive for uniformity and standardization of philosophical approach, of curriculum, of instructional process, of organizational structure, and of physical facilities, there is simply no way that such a system can allow, much less encourage and sustain, the constantly inventive search for new and more productive ways to educate that any truly adaptive educational system must exhibit.

Indeed, our present system rules out the possibility of cultural educational evolution. In the natural world, Darwinian evolution requires a wide diversity of alternative varieties within a species for natural selection to operate and select the one or ones that will best "fit" (i.e., are best adapted to) new environmental circumstances and will thus survive as the sole representatives of a new species.

Similarly, cultural evolution requires a broad diversity of possibilities within any social institution from which it can select the one or ones best adapted to new and ever changing historical circumstances and will thus emerge as the dominant forms. In the case of the American system of public education, which must always operate within a democratic political system, this means that there cannot and should not be any single approach, any single way of educating the young, that is arbitrarily imposed on all students, all parents, all schools, and all school systems, as is the case with the current No Child Left Behind (NCLB) model. And that includes the developmental approach being advocated here.

Rather, it means that we must deliberately create a system of public education that offers its clients and practitioners a wide range of different kinds of schooling, running from very traditional models to very progressive ones, from which both parents and school people can choose the one they believe to be best for the particular children in their care.

Having provided the necessary variation, what we can then hope for—and possibly expect—is that such a system will allow cultural evolution to happen. As our scientific knowledge continues to accumulate, it will (in theory, at least) exert increasing selective pressure on the system to move in more progressive directions. We can then hope that the developmental model, increasingly supported by such knowledge, will prove to be the model best adapted to the unpredictable future that lies ahead of us.

An Adaptive System of Diversity and Choice

In short, we will need to make available to public school parents close to *the full range of legitimate educational options that are now available only to private school parents.* I do not mean that the public system will be able to offer its clients and practitioners an equivalent of the elite, highly selective, antidemocratic private boarding schools such as Groton, Exeter, and Andover, with total yearly costs running as high as those charged by most elite colleges and universities. Nor can any public system offer schools that are overtly religious or sectarian in any fashion.

Nor do I mean that school districts should be allowed to offer schools that are manifestly harmful to children, schools that have been turned into NCLB academic test-prep factories where, for instance, kindergarten children are forced to submit to academic test-prep lessons (I am assuming here, of course, that NCLB has been radically reformed if not entirely abandoned). It is possible—though far from easy—to run traditional, academically oriented schools that are not abusive, that do pay attention to the needs of individual students and treat poor, minority, and special needs students with kindness and respect.

The range of legitimate options to be offered in this new system—if parents and teachers wish them to be offered—can and should run the full gamut from E. D. Hirsch's traditional core knowledge schools on to traditional academic "prep" schools; continuous-progress schools; two-way bilingual schools; the developmental schools such as the Paideia, Waldorf, Montessori, open education/integrated-day, and microsociety schools advocated here. The gamut should also include schools with curricular specialties such as the fine and performing arts, science and technology, the humanities, and global studies.[60]

In addition to the underlying necessity for cultural evolution, there are many immediate, purely pragmatic reasons for creating and practicing such educational diversity and choice. Perhaps one of the most important of these is that it is one of the best ways—if not the best way—to retain both parents and our best teachers and principals in the public system.

As George Tsapatsaris, the project director and superintendent of the Lowell system during the period of planning and creating its system of diversity and choice, has put it:

> In a democracy, you can't just tell people what's good for them and then impose it on them whether they want it or not. Yet that's what we have done in public education. That's why so many parents want to take their children out of the public schools and put them in private or parochial schools. And the same thing applies to teachers and principals.[61]

Seymour Fliegel, a former deputy superintendent in New York City's Community School District 4 in East Harlem, where diversity and choice were pioneered, takes a similar view:

> The aim of [District 4] has been to create a system that—instead of trying to fit students into some standardized school—has a school to fit every student in this district. No kid gets left out, no kid gets lost [and, one might insert here, no child ever gets left behind]. Every kid is important, every kid can learn if you put him or her in the right environment. But since kids have this huge range of different needs, different interests and different ways of learning, we've got to have a wide diversity of schools.[62]

As for teachers, the late Mary Romer, who once served as an assistant to Fliegel, put it this way:

> The fact that we were able here in District Four to treat teachers as adult professionals and give them a chance to do what they've always believed should be done has helped prevent teacher burnout and kept many of the best teachers in our schools.
>
> I was a teacher here in District Four, and let me tell you I would have been long gone if I hadn't had a chance to work in the kind of school I believed in. And this is true for most of the teachers in our schools.[63]

District 4 went about creating diversity by actively encouraging teachers in the system, assisted by parents and community groups, to create new schools. The purpose of this strategy was to enable these small core groups of educationally like-minded professionals and interested parents, all of whom shared a sense of what each new school's mission should be, to create the kinds of schools they believed would provide the best possible education for at least one segment of the district's students. And given the power to create such schools, these small groups of like-minded professionals and parents were not, of course, going to create uniformly similar schools. Since there is that broad diversity of opinions and beliefs about the best way of creating and running schools, teachers and parents will inevitably create (and did create in District 4) a broad diversity of different kinds of schools.

As one example of how such variety can produce the kind of cultural selection desired here, it was in District 4 that Deborah Meier was encouraged to create her developmental Central Park East Elementary School and her 400-student developmental Central Park East High School. These schools have been so successful that the elementary school has been cloned several times, and there are now more than 100 versions of the high school operating in the city.

The "magic" that underlies the success of District 4 is that the district was able to create a situation in which individual schools could be created and chosen by both parents and teachers because they all agreed on what the mission of the school should be and thus on the kind of education the school would offer. Instead of wasting enormous quantities of time and energy attempting to get the randomly mismatched inhabitants of neighborhood schools to agree on a mission, these schools can immediately get down to the business of implementing their own particular vision of educational excellence.

The creation of such a broad diversity of new schools as opposed to attempting to change or reform existing schools is one of the most crucial aspects of District 4's revolution. As Meier puts it, "Such new schools are important because it takes six generations to change existing schools and we haven't got time for that."[64]

Anyone who has actually tackled the job of attempting to transform an already existing, nonchoice, nonmagnet, noncharter neighborhood school knows that it is almost impossible. When everyone has simply been assigned to such a school by the central administration either on the basis of student/parent residence or simply to achieve racial and ethnic balance or because a staff opening just happens to exist there and a teacher is now first on the teacher seniority list, it is utterly impossible for the inhabitants of such a school even to agree on what the school's existing mission is, much less to band together to create a radically new and different one.

What Fliegel and the District 4 people advocate is that every local school district, through this process of continually creating new schools, should gradually replace all its existing nonchoice schools with new choice schools, each of which has a clear and shared sense of its educational mission.

Meier gives a further reason for creating a system of diversity and choice:

> We need schools of choice for all children and parents, first as a means toward family/school trust. A system of choice offers a way of providing for increased professional decision-making without pitting parents and professionals against each other in a power struggle. Schools of choice—if they are small schools—

can offer vastly more time for parents, teachers, and students to meet together—a practice that should be insured by legislation mandating employers to provide time off for parents to attend school meetings.

Schools cannot accomplish this collective task without the support and trust of the student's family. Such trust is not a luxury. Young people sent to school with a message of distrust for the motives and methods of the school are crippled. They must step warily around what the teacher says, looking for hidden traps. Teachers, too, send out mixed messages: On the one hand if you don't behave I'll tell your mother and on the other the values of your family won't get you anywhere.

Teachers rate "parental indifference" to school as their number one complaint. But unless and until parents and teachers join together as advocates for the common good of youngsters, we will not create serious educational breakthroughs for precisely those children we are most concerned about.[65]

Beginning in the 1990s, Boston also took steps toward creating such a new system. Over the past 15 years, the system has created 17 new small, educationally diverse elementary and secondary "pilot" schools, with curricular and staffing autonomy, including an elementary school started by Meier herself, and now serving some 5,900 students.[66] In New York, as mentioned, more than 100 small high schools have been created using the Central Park East model but providing a wide range of differing educational approaches.

All these schools of choice, however, are currently threatened by the NCLB standards and testing juggernaut with its enormous pressures toward uniformity. We are still a long way from having an entire school system built upon the idea of making every school a strictly public, in-district pilot or charter school, that is, a genuinely autonomous school of choice that is voluntarily and collaboratively created by teachers, parents, and students and then freely selected by those and other parents, students, and teachers, a system, in short, in which cultural evolution might actually happen.

Determining What People Want

In other school districts, such as those of Lowell and Worcester, Massachusetts, several of us who had been advocating this system of educational diversity and choice for some years had a chance in the 1980s and 1990s to try a slightly different approach to its creation, the one that was mentioned briefly in the description of Lowell's City and Arts magnet schools.

When we first began to work in these two cities, both of them were under orders from the state to desegregate their de facto segregated school systems. This was only a few years after the court-ordered, "forced busing" desegregation of the nearby Boston schools had produced the widely publicized riots outside South Boston High School. Both parents and professionals in the two systems were deeply concerned about the possibility that such disastrous events might happen in their cities.

Building on the magnet school ideas that had emerged in Boston from the Trotter experience, we suggested first to the Lowell system in 1981 and later to Worcester that the best way both to achieve peaceful desegregation and simultaneously improve the system was to give parents the ability to specify and then choose the kind of schooling their children would receive and give teachers and principals the ability to choose the schools they wished to work in. Such parental choice would have to be "controlled" (i.e., limited) to make sure that all such choices would produce the integrated student bodies required by state law and the federal constitution.

We quickly discovered that the idea that a public school system might offer its parents and practitioners a range of different kinds of schools was pretty much a brand-new idea not only to almost all the parents but to most of the professionals in the system as well. Neither group thought that a public school system could actually offer anything but a standardized school with all important decisions made by the central authorities.

The parents assumed that if they wanted to—or had to—use the public system they would have to send their children to their neighborhood school. If they wanted to choose the kind of schooling they wanted for their children, they assumed that they would have to somehow afford private schooling. The teachers and principals similarly assumed that if they wanted to have any real power to decide how they would conduct their professional lives they too would have to move to the private system.

The planning model we proposed and helped George Tsapatsaris institute in Lowell was that the system should first request and receive from state and the federal Magnet School Assistance Program the funding that would enable the system to set up a citywide Parent Planning Council, made up of two parents elected from the parent body of each elementary and junior high school in the district. It was the job of these representatives not just to serve on the council but also to report all the council's activities back to the parent and professional bodies in their schools. We made sure as well that the council included representatives of both the teacher and administrator unions. Indeed, since many of the teachers had children in the Lowell schools, some of them became "parent" representatives on the council.

The council, assisted by us "outside experts," began its work by plunging into the task of learning about and discussing the various kinds of magnet schools that had been and were being created around the country in such cities as Boston (the three subsystem schools); St. Paul and Minneapolis, Minnesota; and Buffalo, New York.

As this part of the process proceeded, teams of parents and teachers were put on airplanes and visited those magnets all across the country. These teams came back convinced that it really was possible for a public school system to offer choices and that they as parents and teachers very much wanted their system to provide such choice. And they agreed that the provision of such choices, even though they had to be "controlled," was the only way a system such as theirs was going to be peacefully and productively desegregated without the massive White, middle-class flight that occurred in Boston.

The next step in the planning process was for the council members to decide on five or six magnet choices they believed that most Lowell parents would want. The choices they selected here the expected range of very traditional, to open, integrated-day, Montessori, and microsociety models, plus some curricular specialties, such as the fine and performing arts and science and technology. They then prepared surveys of all elementary and junior high parents in the system. The surveys asked parents if they would be willing to have their children bused, to get them to the chosen school. Members of the council then held meetings in all the elementary and junior high schools to inform both parent and teachers of the options they had selected to be on the surveys and to explain in detail exactly what the options were. The surveys were, of course, prepared and then distributed in all appropriate parental languages.

This same Parent Planning Council study and survey process was conducted a year later in Worcester, but with the additional factor of including all elementary and junior high teachers and principals in the surveys.

When these surveys were conducted back in the 1980s in these two cities, many people in both systems thought that many parents might not be prepared (or knowledgeable enough) to make such choices, with some school system people predicting that the return rate would be fairly low, perhaps as low as 10% of each city's total public school parental population. We also were warned that if the parents did choose, they would obviously select mostly the good, old-fashioned, highly academic, back-to-basics industrial model schools they were accustomed to and that teachers and principals might well be the only ones who might choose the more innovative, progressive models. Some people made a further prediction that not only would parents select largely traditional schools but also poor and minority parents would be even less inclined or less able to choose a school and when they did they would be more likely to choose those traditional schools than would nonminority middle-class parents. We were also warned that many parents, even if they chose a school, would not want their children bused.

Not one of these expectations turned out to be the case, surprising even us optimistic "experts." The Worcester surveys, for instance, produced parent return rates that never dropped below 50% when the results were properly analyzed and at times ran as high as 80%. And in both cases, both minority and nonminority parents responded in almost exactly in the same proportions as they were represented in the total parent population.

Further, the models most requested by parents were not good old-fashioned schools concentrating only on the teaching of "the basics." In Lowell, as already mentioned, the two most popular models were the fine and performing arts and microsociety schools, both of which were then created. In Worcester, many parents, both minority and majority, selected a Montessori school (which was not created, because no teachers volunteered to teach in one). And most—but not all—parents answered "yes" or "maybe" to having their children bused (64% in Worcester, for instance).

And also, by substantial margins, it was the parents in both cities who wanted the more adventurous, innovative models and the teachers and principals who wanted the more traditional schools. Not only that, but it was the poor and minority parents, rather than the White, middle-class parents, who more often selected the more progressive models.

Just why these findings were the case we were unsure. When we thought about it later and did ask some questions of both parents and teachers, the best answers we could come up with were that parents simply had learned a great deal during the planning process and discovered that they really did want to have a range of schools from which to choose. The teachers, by contrast, seemed far more cynical—they knew that it was unlikely that any typical American school system would ever really offer them choices.

Needless to say, the choice systems planned and partly instituted by these two school districts have been wiped out (as the case of the City Magnet in Lowell demonstrates) by a combination of the NCLB agenda and a mandated Massachusetts state system of high-stakes standardized testing that has put every public school in the state in a curricular and pedagogical straitjacket, forcing them to concentrate on endless test preparation rather than on unfettered, creative intellectual exploration.

Diversity and Choice as a Process of Research, Development, and Cultural Selection

On the surface, a system of genuine public school diversity and choice can all too easily appear to be—and all too often has been touted as—an expression of the good old capitalistic notion of the all-encompassing virtues of unconstrained competition, a battle between schools for the hearts and most especially the minds and allegiance (and perhaps the money) of any district's parents and students. Out of such social Darwinian warfare for survival, it is predicted, truth, beauty, and good schools will emerge.

But that is by no stretch of anyone's imagination what a good choice system is or should be all about. The initial purpose of a carefully designed and operated system of educational diversity and choice is precisely what George Tsapatsaris and Sy Fliegel claim it to be—a system designed to provide a diversity of schools to meet the wide diversity of student needs and interests and to empower both parents and teachers democratically to select the kinds of schooling they believe will be best for the children in their care. The point of conducting those parent and professional surveys is not to get schools competing with one another but to make sure that the system is providing the full range of educational choices parents and professional people believe they should have.

The ultimate aim of such a choice system, however, is to create an organizational situation in which cultural evolution can occur, a system of continuous educational research and development. Because this new system is an open one, because no parent is ever forced to send his or her child to a school where that child is going to be a guinea pig in some Frankensteinian educational experiment (as the old scare tactic has it) and no teacher is forced to practice a form of schooling he or she does not believe in, like-minded parents; professional staff members; and people from the larger community, including college and university people, can be encouraged to join together to create and try out new and possibly more adaptive models of schooling.

As good biologically based progressive educators, we have to promote the idea that any truly democratic system of public education must be seen as a culturally evolving social mechanism. We must acquire and cling to the faith that our biologically based, developmental educational approach will in good Darwinian fashion and in the longest of runs be culturally selected as the "fittest," in the sense that it will eventually be seen as the system that is best suited to contributing to the survival and improvement of American culture—and therefore possibly even of world culture as well.

Indeed, it is only through such a process of cultural selection that the eventual goal of a system in which all schools are developmental can be realized. If parents and professional staff have the power to choose the kind of schooling they believe is best, some schools will be chosen and some will not. Schools that turn out to be widely popular will have to be cloned—Debbie Meier's Central Park East Elementary has been cloned twice and, as noted earlier, there are now those more than 100 new small high schools in New York City roughly modeled on Central Park East Secondary School.

Other schools, if they are not functioning successfully and are believed by parents and teachers to be failing, will not be chosen at all and will have to go out of business (this, too, has happened, in District 4).[67]

This process of cultural/educational selection, properly conducted, constitutes that continuing and continuous search for more powerful and adaptive forms of education and a gradual abandonment of those that prove to be inappropriate and nonadaptive.

The New Role of Such "R & D"

If such a process of cultural/educational selection is to succeed, every school system's current department or office of "curriculum and instruction" must be transformed into a department or office of educational research and school development. The first job of such a department is to conduct annual parent/professional surveys to determine the degree of parent/professional satisfaction with what is going on in the district, to determine the kinds of schools parents and teachers want (in the initial design stage), and in subsequent years the need for any additional schools not yet created.

A second task of this new department is to assist those teachers, principals, and parents who have an idea for a new school to make that vision come true—to help them design their school, build its educational program, and establish its peculiarly appropriate system of assessment.

This department would then help the new-school people staff their school with like-minded teachers, provide all the necessary facilities and materials with which to start it, assist in the recruitment of like-minded students and parents, and then make sure that each such fledgling school is properly nurtured and protected from bureaucratic and other kinds of interfering predators until it is fully and fairly established, until it is mature enough to fly on its own.

A third task of this office is always to be aware of and actually working with all those researchers on the cutting edge of research in the human cognitive sciences and child and adolescent development. As this research progresses and appears to be producing ideas and strategies that warrant being tested out in the real world of public schooling, it is then the task of the research and school development office to create the conditions for that testing—which in most cases will mean creating entirely new schools in which such testing can have a fair chance of succeeding—as was the case with Boston's subsystem.

Some Further Requirements of Such an Ideal School System

One of the essential principles of the approach to educational reform advocated here is that all schools, in addition to being new schools, should also be either small schools in and of themselves or large schools broken down into small subschools. And all these new small schools must essentially be strictly public "charter" schools having the administrative, curricular, staffing, and fiscal autonomy necessary to guarantee that the school has the freedom to pursue its particular mission, its special approach to the education of children and young people. According to Meier,

> We need small schools so that democratic governance systems become possible. Small schools appear impossible to us because we are usually thinking of our typical big buildings with huge staffs. But just as the Empire State Building contains hundreds of companies, so could all of our big school buildings contain many schools, They could contain schools with different age groups and varying styles and ways of organizing. These small schools could share some facilities such as gym, labs, auditorium, and occasional personnel. They might hire a building manager to coordinate everything as does the Empire State Building.

The educational life of each school, she explains, would remain distinct and independent. Simple changes that would be impossible to make in a big school could be decided upon around a table one afternoon and implemented the very next day in a small school. No school should be larger than 500 students, including high schools. Meier continues:

> Teachers will not have a major impact on the way kids use their minds until they come to know how their students' minds work—student by student. They cannot help young people make sense of things if they do not have time to answer their questions. They cannot improve a student's writing if there isn't time to read it, reflect on it, and then meet occasionally with the student about his or her work. They cannot find ways to connect new ideas with old ones if they have no control over curriculum or pacing. Nor can they influence the values and aspirations of young people if they cannot shape the tone and value system of their classroom and school. To do this they need the power to reorganize the school, the curriculum, the use of time and the allotment of resources at the school level.[68]

To make matters even more democratic, every school of choice in the new school system structure should be governed not by the old autocracy of central administration and principal but by elected boards made up of the school's principal, elected parent representatives, elected teacher representatives, and representatives from the surrounding community.

Parents and the surrounding community are thus empowered to have a voice in the actual running of the school that they as parents have chosen for their children. Community people who are interested in ways the school and the community can serve each other for the betterment of all concerned are also empowered to play a role in creating a school program that will accomplish those particular ends. And, oddly enough, in many of these new kinds of developmental schools, there is—as there must be—a room set aside as a parent, family, and community center, a place where parents, children, and community members are actually welcomed and encouraged to become an integral part of the school's life.

The final task not just of an office of research and school development but of the entire central administrative apparatus is to assist individual schools and the system as a whole to collaborate with all the private, public, civic, social, educational, and community organizations that are needed to turn conventional schools into school/community learning centers and to create those City as Educator and Career Development Center networks that allow our children and young people to learn out in the larger society.

As Jeremy Rifkin puts it in his book *The End of Work*, our students desperately need the "opportunity for deep participation in the community" that "helps engender a sense of personal responsibility and accountability, fosters self-esteem and leadership, and, most of all, allows feelings of creativity, initiative, and empathy to grow and flourish."

It is through such community involvement, says Rifkin, that we can create

> an essential antidote to the increasingly isolated world of simulation and virtual reality children experience in the classroom and at home in front of the television and at their computer work stations. . . . Such involvement can give a youngster a sense of place and belonging, as well as add meaning to his or her life—all of which reverberates back into the classroom, creating a more responsive and motivated student.[69]

But What About "Accountability"?

But what about those loud cries for "accountability," for a national curriculum, for raising those national and state "world class" academic standards, and especially for a national system of tests to find out if all students are meeting those arbitrary standards? Since these cries are not likely to disappear any time soon and since some form of accountability will always be needed, the new school system envisioned here must have an office of student and school accomplishment that is closely coordinated with the office of research and school development.

One of the first tasks of this office is to set up a system for the individual tracking of each and every student in the system, with each student having his or her own identification number and an individual, computerized, developmental portfolio. No matter how many times a student moves within the system, this portfolio of student accomplishment moves as well. This portfolio contains a complete developmental record of what each student has done each year, what the student's developmental successes have been, what things still need to be worked on, the results of any standardized or nonstandardized tests that may have been used, and all teacher and parent comments on the student's progress, with the portfolio always available for parent inspection. The portfolio would also be always available to the student him- or herself with the opportunity for the student to make any and all comments on what it contains.

What this portfolio results in after 12 years of schooling is a comprehensive curriculum vitae or résumé that can then be used to guide student and parent decision making about future schooling and as the basis for a school's recommendations to any and all institutions of higher education.

In addition to this system of student accomplishment, this office would also have the responsibility for tracking the accomplishments of each and every individual school in the system. Here are the key elements of such a school "accountability" plan developed cooperatively by FairTest and the Coalition for Authentic Reform in Education (CARE), an organization made up of reform-minded parents and school people throughout Massachusetts:

1. Local school assessments based upon plans developed and approved by each individual school and each individual school district. Each such individual school plan would spell out the school's mission, that is, its definition of what it hopes to accomplish for its students (including such things as assisting the development of their ability to reason well), how it proposes to assess student progress in these matters and how to report such progress to parents, the school district, and the state; how all decisions will be made, such as those of grade promotion and graduation; and how tests will be used.
2. Limited standardized testing in literary and numeracy only. Test result information used as only one source of data about individual, classroom, and school performance.
3. School-quality reviews every 4 to 5 years, including a detailed self-study followed by visits and a report by teams of independent experts.
4. Annual school reports detailing school progress, or lack of it, to be reviewed by parents, community members, the district, and the state.[70]

The new "open" educational system described here—the provision of a diversity of small schools, parent and professional choice, and school autonomy—actually renders the creation of more elaborate accountability schemes involving uniform state or national standards and crippling "high stakes" state or national tests not only unwise but also unnecessary.

Under this system, the primary method of accountability is simply whether any individual school is able to maintain the commitment of its parents and professional staff, which, as it happens, is the precisely the test of accountability employed by private schools. If the school's parents believe that the school is carrying out its stated mission in a satisfactory fashion and decide to keep their children in that school, then the school has clearly passed the most important accountability test. If the parents are dissatisfied with the school's performance, if they withdraw their children and choose another school they believe will better serve them and their children, then the school is manifestly not succeeding.

In a similar fashion, if the professional staff members of a school believe the school is at least moving in directions they approve of and therefore they choose to remain a part of that school's staff, then again the school has successfully passed that crucial test.

Local school districts will, of course, need to set up that office of student and school accomplishment to make sure that individual schools are successfully fulfilling this fundamental accountability criterion. If a school is failing to do so, then it is the responsibility of the local district to close it down and replace it with a model that might succeed.

This, then, is the second task of the office of student and school accomplishment—to determine whether each school is meeting the performance standards described in the school's mission statement. Each local district must also oversee all schools to ensure fiscal responsibility and must also enforce all general obligatory civil rights rules that prevent racial segregation, as in the creaming off of "easy to reach" students; all rules that prevent political, racial, or religious bias (such as the "teaching" of creationism or intelligent design); and those that ensure basic safety standards.

The New Structures

Meier sums up these new organizational structures when she says, "We need a revolutionary reorganization of our schools and then we need to stand aside, providing the parties to schooling—parents, students, and teachers—with as much help and advice as we can as they work out ways to educate all their children." She goes on:

> Hard won though these reforms may be, they will merely lay the groundwork for slow and steady real change. Some claim we can't afford slow and steady changes. They are wrong. There is nothing faster. The longer we delay the needed structural first steps, the longer

it will take us to begin making use of the vastly increased knowledge we already have on how to help all children learn, knowledge that can only be useful to teachers with professional power and responsibilities backed by supportive families.

We cannot afford to delay. We are wasting resources in expensive research and costly innovations trying to find ways to "motivate" students and teachers. The new "motivators" always presume the need for outside carrots and sticks—imposed merit pay schemes, teacher-retesting mechanisms, endless student testing, automatic test-triggered holdover schemes. But schools of choice, small and highly personal environments, deal with motivation in a completely different way. Professionals can devise their own rewards and their own career ladders. As we bemoan financial abuses or the irregularities of corrupt bureaucrats, professionals, or lay boards, we devise prevention schemes that entail adding new layers of bureaucracy on top of old.

In small professionally run schools, teachers can use resources efficiently because they are natural conservers when it comes to their own materials and eagle-eyed protectors when they understand the school's budget. And parents with a voice in both choosing a school and in the life of that school will be the best monitors of its financial and personal integrity. A school small enough for everyone to know each other is also harder to "hide" in. While some abuses may exist, they would be fewer than now with our vast systems of controllers, monitors, and auditors.

Vandalism, assault, truancy, and apathy on the part of students— these cannot be eliminated by more of the same anonymity of students—metal detectors, ID cards, automated lateness calls, automatic expulsions and holdovers. Vandalism, assault, truancy, and apathy require an assault by school people on the culture of anonymity that permeates our youngsters' lives. Our children need stable personal relationships more than ever, and our schools offer less than ever.[71]

Meier then asks the inevitable question not only about her recommendations but also about everything that has been advocated in this book: Is all this hopelessly utopian, totally unrealistic in a contemporary American society in which so many of our urban and rural school systems are riddled with Jonathan Kozol's "savage inequalities"? School districts where the overcrowded school buildings are filthy and crumbling, where there are few books and no school libraries, where overworked and scandalously underpaid teachers have to spend their own money to buy students pencils and paper, districts that in order to get the feeble funding provided by NCLB must spend millions of their own dollars on testing, districts where our poor and minority children are subjected to endless test prep without a hope that such abusive practices are going to do them anything but educational harm?

And the conservative pundits say that money is not the problem, that it is simply a matter of students and teachers pulling up their frayed socks and working their butts off to raise the academic achievement levels (i.e., the test scores) of our poor and minority students and thus close "the achievement gap."

The situation is not that much better in our wealthy suburbs. The frantic quest for high SAT scores and the expensive tutoring to get them, the hiring of consultants to build impressive noncurricular portfolios to get students into Ivy League universities, the cheating on essays and on exams whenever possible—what does all this have to do with education?

So, in short and finally, we do need to reinvent our system of American public education. We need Meier's "revolutionary reorganization of our schools" and Beck's "genuine social, political and educational revolution in contemporary American society" with his added investment of 8 to 10% of the gross national product.

"Utopian?" asks Meier. "Far less so than the dream that drives it—that all our children can become educated to become the thoughtful citizens a strong democracy needs." So yes, we do need to create a system of schooling that is carefully crafted to serve all the country's children and young people, rich and poor, majority and minority, whether they be foreign or natively born. It will have to be an educational system that is aimed at helping all our children become intelligent, competent, caring adults who understand what makes that larger social world out there tick, who are concerned about the fate of the natural world and all the living creatures in it, people who not only want to change both the social and natural worlds for the better but also are intellectually and emotionally capable of doing something about it.

Suggested Readings

Bracey, G. (2001). *The war against America's public schools: Privatizing schools, commercializing education*. Boston: Allyn & Bacon.

Bracey, G. (2003). *On the death of childhood and the destruction of the public schools: The folly of today's education policies and practices*. Portsmouth, NH: Heinemann.

Bracey, G. (2004). *Setting the record straight: Responses to misconceptions about public education in the U.S.* Portsmouth, NH: Heinemann.

Clinchy, E. (Ed.). (1997). *Transforming public education: A course for America's future*. New York: Teachers College Press.

Clinchy, E. (Ed.). (1999). *Reforming American education from the bottom to the top*. Portsmouth, NH: Heinemann.

Clinchy, E. (Ed.). (2000). *Creating new schools: How small schools are changing American education*. New York: Teachers College Press.

Clinchy, E. (2002). *The rights of all our children: A plea for action*. Portsmouth, NH: Heinemann.

Clinchy, E., & Young, T.W. (1992). *Choice in public education*. New York: Teachers College Press.

Emery, K., & Ohanian, S. (2004). *Why is corporate America bashing our public schools?* Portsmouth, NH: Heinemann.

Featherstone, J. (1971). *Schools where children learn*. New York: Norton.

Fried, R. (2001). *The passionate teacher: A practical guide* (2nd Ed.). Boston, MA: Beacon Press.

Fried, R. (2002). *The passionate learner: How teachers and parents can help children reclaim the joy of discovery*. Boston, MA: Beacon Press.

Fried, R. (2005). *The game of school: Why we play it, how it hurts kids, and what it will take to change it*. San Francisco: Jossey-Bass.

Gardner, H. (1993). *Frames of mind: The theory of multiple intelligences*. New York: Basic Books.

Gardner, H. (2000). *The disciplined mind: Beyond facts and standardized tests, the K–12 education that every child deserves*. New York: Penguin.

Gardner, H. (2004). *The unschooled mind: How children think and how schools should teach*. New York: Basic Books.

Gardner, H. (2006). *Multiple intelligences: New horizons in theory and practice*. Boston, MA: Persons.

Herndon, J. (1981). *How to survive in your native land*. New York: Simon and Schuster.

Holt, J. (1995). *How children fail* (Rev. ed.). New York: Perseus.

Kohl, H. (1988). *36 children*. New York: Penguin.

Kohn, A. (1999). *Punished by rewards: The trouble with gold stars, incentive, plans, A's, praise, and other bribes*. Boston: Houghton Mifflin.

Kohn, A. (2000). *The schools our children deserve: Moving beyond traditional classrooms and "tougher" standards*. Boston: Houghton Mifflin.

Kozol, J. (1990). *Death at an early age: The destruction of the hearts and minds of Negro children in the Boston public schools*. Boston: Houghton Mifflin.

Kozol, J. (1992). *Savage inequalities: Children in America's schools*. New York: Harper.

Kozol, J. (2005). *The shame of the nation: The restoration of apartheid schooling in America*. New York: Crown.

Martin, J. R. (1993). *Changing the educational landscape: philosophy, women, and curriculum*. New York: Routledge.

Meier, D. (2002). *The power of their ideas: Lessons for America from a small school in Harlem*. Boston: Beacon.

Meier, D.(2003). *In schools we trust: Creating communities of learning in an era of testing and standardization*. Boston: Beacon.

Meier, D., & Wood, G. (Eds.). (2004). *Many children left behind: How the No Child Left Behind Act is damaging our children and our schools*. Boston: Beacon.

Noddings, N. (1992). *The challenge to care in the schools*. New York: Teachers College Press.

Ohanian, S. (1999). *One size fits few: The folly of educational standards*. Portsmouth, NH: Heinemann.

Ohanian, S. (2002). *What happened to recess and why are our children struggling in recess?* New York: McGraw-Hill.

Rothstein, R. (1998). *The way we were?: The myths and realities of America's student achievement*. New York: Century Foundation Press.

Rothstein, R. (2004). *Class and schools: Using social, economic, and educational reform to the Black–White achievement gap*. New York: Teachers College Press.

Sarason, S. (2002). *The skeptical visionary: A Seymour Sarason educational reader* (Robert L. Fried, Ed.). Philadelphia: Temple University Press.

Silberman, C. (1971). *Crisis in the classroom and his open classroom reader*. New York: Random House.

Weber, L. (1971). *The English infant school and informal education*. Englewood Cliffs, NJ: Prentice-Hall.

Notes

1. Darwin, C. (1905), *Life and letters of Charles Darwin*, Francis Darwin, editor, vol. 1, chap. 2 (New York: D. Appleton), pp. 29–30.

2. Gopnik, A. (1999, May 6), "Small wonders," *New York Review of Books* 46, no. 8, p. 2.

3. Cremin, L. (1962), The *transformation of the school* (New York: Knopf), p. 177.

4. See Clinchy, E. (1964), "Yes, but what about Irving Engleman," *Phi Delta Kappan*, April, pp. 542–545.

5. Gell-Mann, M., quoted in Brockman, J., editor (1995), *The third culture* (New York: Touchstone, Simon and Schuster), p. 176.

6. Haroutanian-Gordon, S. (1991), *Turning the soul: Teaching through conversation in the high school* (Chicago: University of Chicago Press) p. 70.

7. Cremin (1962), pp. 252–256; see n. 3 , above.

8. Cremin (1962), p. 339; see n. 3, above.

9. Grahame, K. (2005), *Wind in the willows* (New York, Barnes and Noble Classics Series), chap. 1, p. 8.

10. Donkin, R. (2001), *Blood, sweat, and tears: The evolution of work* (New York: Texieres), p. 163.

11. Duckworth, E. (1987), *The having of wonderful ideas and other essays* (New York: Teachers College Press).

12. Duckworth, E. (1991), *Twenty four, forty two, and I love you: Keeping it complex, Harvard Educational Review, 61*, pp. 1–24.

13. Roosevelt, F. (1937), *Second Inaugural Address*, January 20 (New Haven: Avalon Project, Yale University Law School), p. 4.

14. Ulich, R., editor, (1954), *Three thousand years of educational wisdom* (Cambridge, MA: Harvard University Press), p. 463.

15. Wallace, A. R. (1905), *My Life: A record of events and opinions*, vol. 1, pp. 50–51.

16. Ulich (1954), p. 464; see n. 14, above.

17. Tarule, R. (2004), *The artisan of Ipswich* (Baltimore: Johns Hopkins University Press).

18. Maxwell, W., quoted in Bracey, G. (2002), *The war against America's public schools* (Boston: Allyn to Bacon), p. 36.

19. Addams, J. quoted in Curti, M. (1959) *The social ideas of American educators* (Toronto: Littlefield, Adams), p. 203.

20. See Tyack, D. (1974), *The one best system: a history of American urban education* (Cambridge, MA: Harvard University Press).

21. Cremin (1962), pp. 92–93; see n. 3, above.

22. Callahan, R. (1972), *Education and the cult of efficiency* (Chicago: University of Chicago Press).

23. Kramer, M. (2004), *New California wine* (Philadelphia: Running Brook Press), pp. 27–29.

24. Ibid.

25. Callahan (1972), pp. 152; see n. 22, above.

26. See Rothstein, R. (2004), *Class and schools* (New York: Teachers College Press/Economic policy Institute).

27. Ibid.

28. Cremin (1962) pp. 128–135; see n. 3, above.

29. Ibid.

30. Wallace (1905), pp. 98–99; see n. 15, above.

31. See Smith, L. A. H., (1976), *Activity and experience: Sources of English informal education* (New York: Agathon Press). See also Silberman, C. (1973), *Crisis in the classroom*, and Silberman, C., editor, (1973), *The open classroom reader* (New York: Vintage Press).

32. Cremin (1962), pp. 252–256; see n. 3, above.

33. See Gillard, D. (2005), "The Plowden Report," *The Encyclopedia of Informal Education*, fed.org/schooling/plowden_report.htm.

34. Smithers, R. (2006), "Teachers propose scrapping of national curriculum," April 11, *Education Guardian*, available at http://education.guardian.co.uk

35. National Commission on Excellence in Education, (1983), *A nation at risk: The imperative for educational reform* (Washington, DC: U.S. Department of Education), pp. 1–10.

36. Olsen, L. (2004), *NCLB bestows bounty on test industry, Education Week*, Dec 1.

37. See the home page of the National Center for Fair and Open Testing (FairTest) for extensive material critical of NCLB.

38. Hess, F., (2003, December 11) *The case for being mean*. Available at http://www.aei.org/publications/pubID.19614/pub_detail.asp

39. FairTest; see n. 37, above.

40. See Bracey books listed in Suggested Readings list.

41. U.S. Department of Education (2004), *Educational Innovator*, newsletter, December.

42. Atlas, R. D. (2004), "Milliken sees the classroom as a profit center," *New York Times*, Business Day, p. 1.

43. Gopnik (1999); see n. 2, above.

44. Gell-Mann (1995); see n. 5, above.

45. Gopnik (1999); see n. 2, above.

46. Gardner, H. (1983), *Frames of mind: The theory of multiple intelligences* (New York: Basic Books).

47. Gardner, H. (1982), *Developmental psychology* (Boston: Little, Brown), pp. 451–452.

48. Gardner, H. (1986), quoted in Daniel Goldman, "Rethinking the value of

intelligence tests," New York Times Education Life Supplement, November 9, p. 23.

49. Gardner (1982), p. 255; see n. 47, above.

50. Richmond, G. (1973), *The microsociety school: a real world in miniature* (New York: Harper & Row).

51. Richmond, G. (1989), "The future school: Is Lowell pointing us toward a revolution in education? *Phi Delta Kappan*, vol. 71, no. 3, November, pp. 227–229.

52. Educational Planning Associates (1972), *The city as educator: Education and the bicentennial* (Boston: Boston Redevelopment Authority, City Hall).

53. Wille, L. (1997), *At home in the Loop: How clout and community built Chicago's Dearborn Park* Carbondale: Southern Illinois University Press), pp. 71, 192.

54. Beck, A. (1997), *The knowledge business: A new song for the choir*, http://www.math.wisc.edu/~beck/kbO.htm, p. 2.

55. Bowen, W. C., Kurzwell, M. A., and Tobin, E. M: (2005), "Equity and excellence in American higher education," *Harvard Magazine*, May–June, pp. 54, 90.

56. Donald, M. (1991), *Origins of the modern mind*, (Cambridge, MA: Harvard University Press), p. 346.

57. Rose, M. (2004), *The mind at work: Valuing the intelligence of the American worker* (New York: Penguin), p. 215.

58. Gell-Mann, M.(1995) quoted in Brockman, J. (1995). pp. 176–179. See n. 5.

59. Meier, D., personal communication, 1998.

60. See Young, T. W. and Clinchy, E. (1993), *Choice in public education* (New York, Teachers College Press).

61. Tsapataris, G. (1987), quoted in Clinchy, E., "An educational renaissance in East Harlem," unpublished paper, Institute for Responsive Education, Boston.

62. Fliegel, S. (1987), quoted in Clinchy, E., "An educational renaissance"; see n. 61, above.

63. Romer, M. (1987), quoted in Clinchy, "An educational renaissance."

64. Meier, D. (1987), quoted in Clinchy, "An educational renaissance."

65. Meier, D. (1987), quoted in Clinchy, "An educational renaissance."

66. French, D. (2006), "Commentary: Boston's pilot schools," *Education Week*, April 19, p. 33.

67. See Clinchy, E., editor (2000), *Creating new schools: How small schools are changing American education* (New York: Teachers College Press).

68. Meier, D. (1987), quoted in Clinchy, "An educational renaissance."

69. Rifkin J. (1996), "Commentary: Rethinking the mission of American education, *Education Week*, January 21, p. 32.

70. FairTest; see no. 37, above.

71. Meier, D. (1987), quoted in Clinchy, "An educational renaissance."

Index

About the Author

Evans Clinchy is Senior Research Associate at the Institute for Responsive Education at Cambridge College in Cambridge, Massachusetts. His strange and idiosyncratic educational career has included service as an educational reporter on a local Connecticut newspaper; as a Nieman Fellow in educational journalism at Harvard University; as an educational program officer at a sub-foundation of the Ford Foundation; as the educational and administrative director of an elementary school social studies curriculum reform program called Man: A Course of Study; as the director of the Office of Program Development in the Boston Public Schools, which included the tasks of creating and directing its K–12 Model Demonstration Subsystem and Educational Planning Center; and as president of Educational Planning Associates, an educational consulting firm.

He has published many articles in *Phi Delta Kappan* and other professional journals and five books: *Transforming Public Education: A Course for America's Future* (editor, 1997); *Creating New Schools: How Small Schools Are Changing American Education* (editor, 2000); *The Rights of All Our Children: A Plea for Action* (2002); *Reforming American Education from the Bottom to the Top* (editor, 1999); and *Choice in Public Education* (with Timothy W. Young, 1992).

He welcomes responses to this book at eclinchysr@yahoo.com.